CAUGHT UP TO HEAVEN

CAUGHT UP TO HEAVEN

Biblical Answers to 80 Questions about Heaven
for Hope and Comfort

Frank R. Shivers

LIGHTNING SOURCE
1246 Heil Quaker Blvd.
La Vergne, TN

Unless otherwise noted, Scripture quotations are from
The Holy Bible *King James Version*

Library of Congress Cataloging-in-Publication Data

Shivers, Frank R., 1949-
Caught Up to Heaven / Frank Shivers
ISBN 978-1-878127-42-6

Library of Congress Control Number:
2020906442

Cover design by
Tim King of North Carolina

For Information:
Frank Shivers Evangelistic Association
P. O. Box 9991
Columbia, South Carolina 29290
www.frankshivers.com

Presented to

_____

By

_____

Date

_____

Then we which are alive and remain
shall be caught up together with them in the clouds,
to meet the Lord in the air: and so shall we ever be with
the Lord.
~ 1 Thessalonians 4:17

To

Robert Jumper

Robert, a superb singer and music director and close friend, has worked with me in revival meetings and camps throughout the years. Few men possess the gift not only to arouse a congregation to engage in worship through singing and set "the table" for the minister to preach the Word, but as "soloist" to magnify and glorify Christ, stirring hearts to do likewise. Robert epitomizes all three.

It is fitting this book be dedicated to him, for he often refreshed my soul and that of saints in attendance in our revivals with songs about Heaven's beauty, magnificence, and splendor, stimulating excitement and praise. Songs like "Beulah Land," "The King Is Coming," "Precious Lord, Take My Hand" and "The Sweet By and By," none can sing better.

With delight I recall "Bob" singing to children at one of our camps:

Heaven is a wonderful place,
Filled with glory and grace.
I wanna see my Savior's face,
'Cause Heaven is a wonderful place.
I wanna go there! ~ O. A. Lambert

Thank you, "Bob," for nearly a lifetime of fellowship and the many years of partnership in the gospel ministry. It's been an awesome journey together.

Aim at Heaven and you will get earth "thrown in": aim at earth and you will get neither.[1] ~ C. S. Lewis

What a Gathering

On that bright and golden morning when the Son of Man shall come
And the radiance of His glory we shall see,
When from ev'ry clime and nation He shall call His people home,
What a gath'ring of the ransomed that will be!

What a gath'ring, what a gath'ring,
What a gath'ring of the ransomed in the summer land of love!
What a gath'ring, what a gath'ring,
Of the ransomed in that happy home above!

When the blest who sleep in Jesus at His bidding shall arise
From the silence of the grave and from the sea,
And with bodies all celestial they shall meet Him in the skies,
What a gath'ring and rejoicing there will be!

When our eyes behold the city, with its many mansions bright,
And its river, calm and restful, flowing free;
When the friends that death hath parted shall in bliss again unite,
What a gath'ring and a greeting there will be!

Oh, the King is surely coming, and the time is drawing nigh
When the blessed day of promise we shall see;
Then the changing "in a moment, in the twinkling of an eye,"
And forever in His presence we shall be.
What a gath'ring, what a gath'ring,
What a gath'ring of the ransomed in the summer land of love!
What a gath'ring, what a gath'ring,
Of the ransomed in that happy home above!

~ Fanny Crosby (1887)

Contents

Preface

An imperative rule for having correct Scripture interpretation and application is to always interpret a text within its context. "A text without a context is a pretext for a proof text." Bible readers, Bible teachers and ministers wade into unfounded and questionable territory in applying a text to a matter to which it does not properly apply. To safeguard against spurious interpretation and application of a verse or passage, a thorough *exegesis* (dissection of the text word by word) and analysis of its context (its connection with surrounding verses and/or other passages in Scripture) are imperative. They provide the necessary check and balance to insure proper interpretation and application. A seemingly apparent meaning and application of a text, if contradicted by other Scripture, is incorrect. Scripture always confirms (supports, undergirds) itself—never otherwise.

Some of our thoughts and beliefs about Heaven (and other great doctrines of the faith) are unfounded due to sincere but spurious interpretation. To *twist* a verse to make it applicable to a subject and/or to be supportive to one's belief is "handling the word of God deceitfully" (2 Corinthians 4:2). W. A. Criswell well states, "Strange notions about Heaven often distort the beauty of this Christian doctrine."[2] Therefore, it is imperative to make sure our "notions" of Heaven are biblically based.

In this volume earnest and unbiased effort was undertaken to ensure that which is stated is in harmony with the whole of God's Word and substantiated through the rule of biblical interpretation previously cited. There are numerous questions about Heaven for which the Bible does not give an answer. When the Bible is silent about a matter, man can only speculate about it—and that's the danger.

To wrestle intensely with Scripture for hours to ascertain its purest meaning has been an invigorating and illuminating feat.

However, despite my best efforts in the endeavor, the reader may find my interpretations flawed. I hope not, but if so, keep in mind that it's the Holy Scriptures that are infallible, not man's commentary upon them.

Introduction

Charles Simeon, a theologian of the 18th century, penned in one sentence the saint's motivation not to be defeated or depressed by the hardships, heartaches and hurtful things of this present life. He wrote, "A hope of future happiness affords strong consolation under present trials."[3] To know that a far better place awaits in the Father's House makes the present suffering and trials endurable. In reference to the believer's hope of Heaven, Paul says, "That's why I don't think there's any comparison between the present hard times and the coming good times. The created world itself can hardly wait for what's coming next. Everything in creation is being more or less held back. God reins it in until both creation and all the creatures are ready and can be released at the same moment into the glorious times ahead. Meanwhile, the joyful anticipation deepens" (Romans 8:18–21 MSG).

The believer is out of place here. It's a place contrary to his beliefs, standards and values. Therefore, he suffers from persecution, opposition, discrimination and being ostracized. Jesus forewarned us to expect all of it. In John 16, He said, "I have told you these things, so that in Me you may have [perfect] peace. In the world you have tribulation and distress and suffering, but be courageous [be confident, be undaunted, be filled with joy]; I have overcome the world" (John 16:33 AMP). And in John 14:27–29, He said, "Peace I leave with you, My peace I give to you; not as the world gives do I give to you. Let not your heart be troubled, neither let it be afraid. You have heard Me say to you, '*I am going away and coming back to you.*' If you loved Me, you would rejoice because I said, 'I am going to the Father,' for My Father is greater than I. And now I have told you before it comes, that when it does come to pass, you may believe" (NKJV).

The saints' present peace and joy are invariably linked to the return of Christ to take them Home. Paul instructs saints to encourage one another by reminding them of the soon coming of the Lord and our exodus Home. He writes, "Brothers and sisters, we want you to know about those Christians who have died so you will not be sad, as others who have no hope. We believe that Jesus died and that he rose again. So, because of him, God will raise with Jesus those who have died. What we tell you now is the Lord's own message. We who are living when the Lord comes again will not go before those who have already died. The Lord himself will come down from Heaven with a loud command, with the voice of the archangel, and with the trumpet call of God. And those who have died believing in Christ will rise first. After that, we who are still alive will be gathered up with them in the clouds to meet the Lord in the air. And we will be with the Lord forever. So encourage each other with these words" (1 Thessalonians 4:13–18 NCV).

In the inspirational book *What to Do Until Jesus Comes Back*, W. A. Criswell states, "We all are going to share in the Kingdom—all of us (saints). There will not be a bone left in the region of death for Satan to gloat over. The Devil will never be able to say, 'This is a part of one of God's children: here is one of his bones in my hand.' No sir! We all shall be resurrected and every part of us quickened."[4] The end of time is in the precious hands of God as much as its beginning was.[5] As He set things in motion, He will wind them down. Look up! Our "redemption draweth nigh" (Luke 21:28). Soon Jesus will come with His ring of keys and say, "It's closing time," and the saints will be raptured Home where they belong. This that He has promised will be our reality when He comes for us! How stupendous is that news! Concentrate on it. Digest it. Consume it. Talk about it. Walk in it. Expect it. Encourage others with it. Joy in it—"Rejoice, because your names are written in Heaven" (Luke 10:20). Stay your mind on the future glory that awaits when Jesus comes for His church.

Joseph Addison tells of a traveler that strayed into the palace of a King to rest, mistaking it for an inn. Upon the plush carpet the man rested until confronted by a palace guard. The king happened to pass through the gallery at the same moment. The king asked the man, "How could you be so stupid as to think that this palace was an inn?"

The man replied, "Let me ask you a question. Who lived here in this house when it was built?"

"My ancestors," was the king's reply.

"And who lived here before you," the traveler further inquired.

The king responded, "My father."

Next, the king was asked by the man, "Who will live here after you?"

The king answered, "My son, the prince."

"Ah, sir," said the man, "a house that changes inhabitants so often is not a palace; it is an inn."[6] Again and again the Bible reminds us this world is not our HOME; it's merely an inn. As saints, we are simply passing through this land on our way to that Land fairer than day.

Banish your cares and concerns for a while. Stop and ponder afresh through the pages of this book the wonders and glory of Heaven. By faith, enter that land; penetrate it and possess it until your heart is inflamed with excitement about it and anticipation for it. See the happiness and peace in that land. See family and friends gathered there in pure delight. See its pristine and immaculate beauty. See what things which brought sorrow and horror on earth are not there. See the "mansions" there. But especially see Jesus clothed in majesty seated upon Heaven's throne!

As I grow older and Home draws nearer, my passion for knowledge about it intensifies and readiness for it multiplies. The labor required in the study, prayer, research, wrestling with texts and writing of this volume has certainly kindled that flame substantially. It is my heartfelt prayer that something that is said within its pages will instill hope, comfort, consolation and peace while providing illumination of the wonder and majestic beauty of Heaven to the reader.

How happy every child of grace
Who knows his sins forgiven!
"This earth," he cries, "is not my place;
"I seek my place in Heaven:

"A country far from mortal sight;
"Yet, oh! by faith I see
"The land of rest, the saints' delight,
"The Heaven prepar'd for me." ~ Charles Wesley (1759)

How to Use This Book

Use it to inflame the heart with excitement and tremendous joy about Heaven.

Use it to minister comfort and solace to the brokenhearted and sorrowing.

Use it to minister hope and peace to the dying.

Use it to console the troubled in heart.

Use it to enlighten saints with knowledge of their eternal home.

Use it as an evangelistic tool to introduce the unsaved to Christ.

Use it to grant assurance that Heaven awaits the saint at life's end.

Use it to rebuff erroneous teaching about Heaven.

Use it to strengthen and increase faith regarding the afterlife of the believer.

Use it in the church, funeral home, nursing home, hospital and hospice.

"As cold waters to a thirsty soul, so is good news from a far country" (Proverbs 25:25). All identify with the Proverb's truth, for all know what it is to wait eagerly and expectantly at the mailbox (computer or phone) for a good word from a family member or friend from a "far country" (locally or globally) until it arrives. The jubilation and refreshment such news bring to the heart is likened to one with parched lips having his thirst satisfied with "cold waters" (plural, i.e., all that he desires).

The good news of the preparation made for the saint's arrival in Heaven, the many loved ones that await his arrival, and the announcement that the King is soon to return to earth are all good news from a far country and are as *cold waters* to a thirsty soul.

Who might be looking to you for that good news from a *far country* to refresh his soul and renew his spirit? Dispense some "cold waters" to his parched lips today by placing a copy of this book in his hand.

Quotations about Heaven from the Pen of Great Saints

"To go to Heaven, fully to enjoy God, is infinitely better than the most pleasant accommodations here."[7] ~ Jonathan Edwards

"It is a sweet thing to die in the Lord: it is a covenant-blessing to sleep in Jesus. Death is no longer banishment; it is a return from exile, a going Home to the many mansions where the loved ones already dwell."[8] ~ C. H. Spurgeon

"We must seek to understand the *biblical* concept of Heaven. We are commanded to contemplate Heaven, to pursue it the way Abraham sought the city of God, to fix affections there."[9] ~ John MacArthur

"The best thing that can happen to you in this life is to grow old in anticipation of what God has in store for you."[10] ~ Jerry Vines

"The world has forgotten, in its concern with Left and Right, that there is an Above and a Below."[11] ~ Glen Drake

"Only in Heaven will we know exactly what Heaven is like."[12] ~ Billy Graham

"This body (in Heaven) dominated by the spirit will be the same body as to identity which we have now but changed as to composition and life principle."[13] ~ Kenneth Wuest

"We are taught to conceive of Heaven as a place of unspeakable felicity (intense happiness). The description given of it by St. John is intended to elevate our thoughts and enlarge our conceptions to the uttermost; but a spiritual mind, which is dead to earthly things, may perhaps see no less beauty in our Lord's description."[14] ~ Charles Simeon

"If you are a Christian, you are not a citizen of this world trying to get to Heaven; you are a citizen of Heaven making your way through this world."[15] ~ Vance Havner

"There is no good in this life but what is mingled with some evil: honors perplex, riches disquiet, and pleasures ruin health. But in

Heaven we shall find blessings in their purity, without any ingredient to embitter, with everything to sweeten them."[16] ~ John Bunyan

"This world is only an anteroom (a smaller room that is the entryway into a larger one) for the next."[17] ~ John R. Rice

"Heaven is a place of ceaseless activity and meaningful responsibility, without the limitations of the space-time-mortality continuum."[18] ~ W. A. Criswell

"There are only two kinds of people in the end: those who say to God, 'Thy will be done,' and those to whom God says, in the end, 'Thy will be done.' All that are in Hell choose it. Without that self-choice there could be no Hell. No soul that seriously and constantly desires joy (*Heaven*) will ever miss it. Those who seek, find. To those who knock, it is opened."[19] ~ C. S. Lewis

1. What Is Heaven?

What is Heaven? It is a place created by God (Acts 4:24). It is a place (John 14:2) of the eternal abode of God (Psalm 11:4; 1 Kings 8:30; Acts 7:55; Matthew 6:9), angels (Mark 13:32) and the saints (Revelation 7:14–15). It is the place from which Jesus left to come to earth in His redemptive mission (John 3:13; 6:33–51). It is the place to which Jesus returned to prepare for the saints (John 14:2). It is the saint's ultimate destination.[20]

It is the place where awesome, inspirational worship occurs at the throne of God (Revelation 5:13–14; 7:9–12) and of joyous delightful service unto the Lord (Revelation 22:3). It is a place of rest; the labor performed does not diminish strength (Revelation 14:3). W. B. Cooke states, "Heaven is a place as well as a state of being."[21] The word "Heaven" is mentioned in the Bible more than 300 times in the Old Testament and more than 200 times in the New Testament (King James Version).

Billy Graham said in the book *World Aflame*: "Heaven will be more modern and up-to-date than any of the present-day constructions of man. Heaven will be a place to challenge the creative genius of the unfettered mind of redeemed man. Heaven will be a place made supremely attractive by the presence of Christ."[22]

It's My Father's House

But it is more than a "place," for Jesus states that Heaven is "My Father's house" (John 14:2). Such knowledge is rapturous to the soul! J. P. Brown says, "Be it what it may and where it may, this vast unknown, it is filled with that nameless benediction, a Father's presence and lit with the light of a Father's smile. It is this sense of a loving Presence meeting us at life's outer gate and bringing us into a bright Home full of light and beauty and living joy which, for the Christian, has so utterly dissipated the terror; and this made

1

death seem to Francis of Assisi as a sister to take him by the hand and conduct him home."[23]

The psalmist said, "Glorious things are spoken of thee, O city of God. Selah" (Psalm 87:3). But as glorious as the old Jerusalem (Zion) was, it fails to compare in the least to the splendor and majestic beauty of the New Jerusalem (Heaven).

"The glories and blessedness of Heaven," writes Arthur Pink, "are brought before us in the New Testament under a variety of representations. Heaven is called a 'country' (Luke 19:12; Hebrews 11:16); this tells of its vastness. It is called a 'city' (Hebrews 11:10; Revelation 21); this intimates the large number of its inhabitants. It is called a 'kingdom' (2 Peter 1:11); this suggests its orderliness. It is called 'paradise' (Luke 23:43; Revelation 2:7); this emphasizes its delights. It is called the 'Father's house' (John 14:2), which bespeaks its permanency."[24]

When all is said and done about Heaven, *"He (Jesus) thinks it ought to be enough to be assured that they (believers) shall be where He is and in His keeping."*[25] Certainly, that is Heaven enough for me. And it was for the prolific songwriter (over 9,000 hymns) Fanny Crosby who became blind at the age of six weeks. A well-meaning minister said to her, "I think it is a great pity that the Master did not give you sight when he showered so many other gifts upon you." "Do you know that if at birth I had been able to make one petition, it would have been that I was born blind?" replied the poet. "Because when I get to Heaven, the first face that shall ever gladden my sight will be that of my Savior."[26]

> Through the gates to the city in a robe of spotless white,
> He will lead me where no tears will ever fall;
> In the glad song of ages I shall mingle with delight;
> But I long to meet my Savior first of all. ~ Fanny Crosby (1891)

> Heaven is a place where we will need nothing more, want nothing more than to worship Jesus for eternity. ~ Adrian Rogers

A little girl was blind from birth and knew the beauties of earth only from the lips of her mother. A skilled surgeon operated on the child's eyes and at last was successful. As the last bandage dropped from her eyes, ecstatically she ran into her mother's arms, then to the window and an open door. As the beauties of God's creation filled her vision, she ran screaming back to her mother, saying, "O Mama, why didn't you tell me it was so beautiful?" The mother, wiping tears from her eyes, replied, "My precious child, I tried to tell you but I couldn't do it."

Upon the day the redeemed get to Heaven, seeing its beauty and glory, I think we will search out John and say, "John, why didn't you tell us it was so beautiful?" And he will respond, "I tried to tell you when I wrote the twenty-first and twenty-second chapters of Revelation after I had my vision of it, but I couldn't do it."[27] The best effort of the most eloquent tongue or prolific pen to describe Heaven touches but the hem of its glorious garment.

2. Is Heaven a Real Place?

Is Heaven a figurative or a literal place? The One who knows (Jesus) states it is a literal place (John 14:2). It is a *place* just as much as the city in which you reside is a place. If it were not, the Bible would not speak of its streets of pure gold, walls of jasper, foundations of twelve precious stones and gates of pearl, or its inhabitants. See Revelation 21:18–21. If Heaven was not a literal domain, Jesus never would have said, "Lay not up for yourselves treasures upon earth, where moth and rust doth corrupt, and where thieves break through and steal: But lay up for yourselves treasures in heaven, where neither moth nor rust doth corrupt, and where thieves do not break through nor steal" (Matthew 6:19–20).

Couple these descriptions of Heaven with its measurement cited in Revelation 21 and 22, and the question of its real, literal existence becomes moot, for such cannot be said of a state of mind. "It is no poet's dream, no fictitious realm."[28] John R. Rice states, "I tell you, Heaven is a real, literal, physical place, a city as material, as physical, as literal as Chicago or London or New York or Tokyo."[29] Its reality is mentioned over 70 times in the Gospel of Matthew alone.

"Much of the secularism and rationalism of our times," states A. W. Tozer, "dismisses the Christian view and teaching about Heaven as nothing more than hopeful thinking. But the Christian's promised *hope of future blessedness is founded upon the fullest and plainest revelations of the Old and New Testaments.* That it accords with the most sacred yearnings of the human breast does not weaken it, but serves rather to confirm the truth of it, because the One who made the heart might be expected also to make provision for the fulfillment of its deepest longings."[30]

To the liberals who claim this description of Heaven is simply figurative language, Jesus responds, "If it were not so, I would have told you" (John 14:2). In other words, Jesus is saying, "If Heaven were not like I described it, I would have told you so!" Believers must remember that besides the little we do know about Heaven, there is far more that we do not know. Paul affirms this truth: "But as it is written, Eye hath not seen, nor ear heard, neither have entered into the heart of man, the things which God hath prepared for them that love him" (1 Corinthians 2:9).[31] The best description of Heaven fails to touch the hem of its awesome glorious garment.

> It is no poet's dream, no fictitious realm.

"To those who doubt the existence of Heaven because, no matter how far we travel in space, we have yet to locate it," says Jon Courson, "consider the following facts. The distance between the electrons and the nucleus of an atom being proportionate to the distance between Pluto and the sun, all matter on this earth is comprised of ninety-five percent space—leaving plenty of room for an unseen dimension to coexist with the material world we presently perceive."[32]

A pastor noted a little boy with arms extended toward the sky holding a string tightly in hands. He inquired, "What are you doing here, my little friend?"

"Flying my kite, sir," he replied.

"Flying your kite!" exclaimed the pastor. "I can see no kite; you can see none."

The boy replied, "I know, sir. I cannot see it, but I know that it there, for *I feel its pull.*"

Though Heaven is not visible from my vantage point, I know that it is there, for I feel its pull!

3. Why Did Jesus Have to Prepare Heaven?

Jesus told the disciples, "I go to prepare a place for you" (John 14:2). What did He mean?

The imagery of Jesus returning to His carpentry skills, pounding nails into boards and constructing houses for believers is spurious.[33] Rather, "it surely describes his death, resurrection, ascension, and princely role at the Father's right hand."[34] His return to Heaven completed the divinely assigned redemptive mission (the final "nail" to be hammered) to make saints ready for Heaven and Heaven ready for them. D. A. Carson agrees, saying the words "presuppose that the 'place' exists before Jesus gets there. It is not that He arrives on the scene and then begins to prepare the place; rather, in the context of Johannine theology, it is the going itself, via the cross and resurrection, [and I add ascension] that prepares the place for Jesus' disciples."[35] Paul explains, "But the glorious fact is that Christ did rise from the dead: He has become the very first to rise of all who sleep the sleep of death. As death entered the world through a man, so has rising from the dead come to us through a Man! As members of a sinful race, all men die; as members of the Christ of God, all men shall be raised to life, each in his proper order, with Christ the very first and after Him all who belong to Him when He comes" (1 Corinthians 15:20–22 PHILLIPS).

> The imagery of Jesus returning to His carpentry skills, pounding nails into boards and constructing houses for believers is spurious.

Arthur Pink further unravels the words "I go to prepare a place for you." He said [my paraphrase]: It means that Jesus has procured the right for every regenerated sinner to enter Heaven by His death on the Cross. He has "prepared" us a place there as our Representative (Forerunner) by planting His royal banner in its soil and procuring it on our behalf. Further, Jesus has "prepared" for us a place there "by entering the 'holy of holies' on High as our great High Priest, carrying our names in with Him." See Hebrews 6:20. Christ did all that was necessary to secure a permanent place in Heaven for His children.[36]

"Christ prepares the place in Heaven for His own, and the Holy Spirit prepares the redeemed on earth for their place in Heaven."[37] After all, Heaven is a prepared place for a prepared people. Apart from Christ's cross, triumphant resurrection and exaltation (redemptive work), no place in Heaven could have been prepared for the sinner.

4. Where Is Heaven?

It may be deduced from Scripture Heaven is "above" the earth. For example, when God chose to stop the building of Babel, He said, "Let us go down" (Genesis 11:7) and Jesus, forty days after His resurrection, was "taken up into Heaven" (Acts 1:9). See John 3:13; Psalm 103:11; Psalm 14:2 and Revelation 4:1. At the rapture of the church the saints will be *snatched up* to meet Jesus in the air (1 Thessalonians 4:17).

I'm going up, up, up;
I'm going up.
Bless the Lord, when Jesus comes,
I'm going up.

When the trumpet shall resound,
In the earth I'll not be found;
In the twinkling of an eye,
I'm going up, up, up. ~ Ethelwyn Robinson Taylor (1939)

Scripture also reveals that Heaven is a fixed location in the sides of the north beyond the highest star.[38] This is based upon Psalm 75:6–7: "Promotion cometh neither from the *east*, nor from the *west*, nor from the *south*. But God is the judge: he putteth down one, and setteth up another." Isaiah 14:12–15 makes clear why the *north* was omitted in that text. "How art thou fallen from heaven, O Lucifer, son of the morning! how art thou cut down to the ground, which didst weaken the nations! For thou hast said in thine heart, I will ascend into heaven, I will exalt my throne above the stars of God: I will sit also upon the mount of the congregation, in the sides of the north: I will ascend above the heights of the clouds; I will be like the most High. Yet thou shalt be brought down to hell, to the sides of the pit."

Heaven, then, is a fixed place in the sides of the north. Isaiah adds that it is located beyond highest star (Isaiah 14:13–14). I agree with B. R. Lakin's conclusion about the matter: "We are not told the exact location of Heaven, but we are content in letting God alone know the whereabouts of our future abode. To know that it exists and that it is our final destination is enough for the trusting child of God."[39]

5. Will We Know Each Other in Heaven?

Paul forthrightly states we will be identifiable in Heaven. "For now we see through a glass, darkly; but then face to face: now I know in part; but then shall I know even as also I am known" (1 Corinthians 13:12).

On the Mount of Transfiguration, Moses and Elijah in their heavenly (resurrected) bodies were recognized by the disciples (Matthew 17:1–4). Mary recognized Jesus in His resurrected body (John 20:16). Jesus said that saints will see "Abraham, and Isaac, and Jacob, and all the prophets, in the kingdom of God" (Luke 13:28), clearly meaning they will be recognizable. A rich man (Dives) sorely treated a beggar named Lazarus at his gate. Upon his death, Lazarus was escorted by the angels to Heaven while the rich man was cast into outer darkness in Hell. From the chambers of Hell, the man recognized Lazarus in Heaven (Luke 16:23). To Mary, the distraught, grieving sister of Lazarus (a different Lazarus than the one in Luke 16), Jesus said, "Thy brother shall rise again" (John 11:23). In death he was yet her brother, and she his sister.

W. A. Criswell, in *Heaven,* states that one's personality survives in Heaven, that we will each be who we are now but without the baggage of sin and imperfection.[40] Further, Criswell states, "We shall not know less of each other in Heaven; we shall know more. We shall possess our individual names in Heaven. We shall be known as individuals. You will be you; I shall be I; we shall be we. Personality and individuality exist beyond the grave."[41]

> We shall not know less of each other in Heaven; we shall know more. We shall possess our individual names in Heaven. We shall be known as individuals. You will be you; I shall be I; we shall be we. Personality and individuality exist beyond the grave. ~ W.A. Criswell

The Bible clearly teaches that your child on earth will be your child in Heaven; and thus, your mother will be your mother, your father be your father, and so on. Obviously, the role in the relationship will change in Heaven, but the relationship will continue.

The dying words of the famed evangelist Dwight L. Moody were: "Earth recedes; Heaven opens before me." His son William, by his bedside, testified that his father also said, "No, this is no dream, Will. It is beautiful. It is like a trance. If this is death, it is sweet. There is no valley here. God is calling me, and I must go." Shortly the entire family joined William at Moody's bedside.

Suddenly Moody's face brightened, and he said, "Dwight! Irene! I see the children's faces!" (Recently his two grandchildren Dwight and Irene had died.)

One family we dwell in Him,
One Church above, beneath,
Though now divided by the stream,
The narrow stream of death. ~ Charles Wesley (1759)

6. How Far Is Heaven?

The nearness of Heaven may be suggested by a "veil," which is the thinnest and frailest of partitions. Presently there is only a "veil" between the saint and Heaven. Though the body is fearfully and wonderfully made, it is as a thin veil, utterly frail. It can snap, break or collapse at any moment. A slight wound of a poisonous thorn, insect bite, breath of an infected person with a communicable deadly disease may suddenly cause the end of earthly life. In the instant that the veil is rent, in the twinkling of an eye, one throbbing beat of the heart, the saint is ushered by angels into Heaven's splendor and to God's throne.[42]

Only faintly now I see Him
With the darkling veil between,
But a blessed day is coming
When His glory shall be seen. ~ Carrie Ellis Breck (1898)

Billy Graham said, "Just because Heaven is beyond the reach of man's satellites and telescopes, however, does not mean that Heaven is beyond the reach of our hearts."[43] "We measure distance by time", says C. H. Spurgeon. "We are apt to say that a certain place is so many hours from us. If it is a hundred miles off and there is no railroad (or car), we think it a long way; if there is a railway (or car), we think we can be there in no time. But how near must we say Heaven is—for it is just one sigh, and we get there."[44]

Heaven is only a short breath away,
So ready your soul without delay.
Let Jesus be your Savior and Lord;
Fit then you'll be to enter its door. ~ Frank Shivers (2020)

> That we are so near death is too good to be believed.
> ~ Henry Ward Beecher

Henry Ward Beecher says, "One should go to sleep at night as homesick passengers (aboard ship) do, saying, 'Perhaps in the morning we shall see the shore.' To us who are Christians, it is not a solemn, but delightful thought that perhaps nothing but the opaque, bodily eye prevents us from beholding the gate which is open just before us and nothing but a dull ear prevents us from hearing the ringing of those bells of joy which welcome us to the Heavenly Land. That we are so near death is too good to be believed."[45]

Two Christians ate healthy during their life. Upon death they went to Heaven. They marveled at its beauty and splendor. One said to the other, "Wow. I never imagined Heaven would be as good as *this!*"

"Yeah," agreed the other. "And just think, if we hadn't eaten all that oat bran, we could have gotten here ten years sooner."[46]

7. What Is the Preeminent Thing about Heaven?

Most conversations and sermons about Heaven focus primarily upon what we get (reunion with family and friends, peace, happiness, rest, deliverance from the tyranny and presence of Satan) or do (worship, work, play). While all these things are "benefits" of the saint's Home (and ought to be talked about and sung about with glee), Scripture places them secondary to that of beholding Jesus, the King of kings and Lord of lords seated upon Heaven's throne. Seeing Jesus is the very first thing John says about our entrance into Heaven: "And *they shall see his face;* and his name shall be in their foreheads" (Revelation 22:4).

Oh, that will be glory for me,
(Oh, that will be glory for me,)
Glory for me, (Glory for me,)
Glory for me! (Glory for me!)
When by His grace I shall look on His face,
That will be glory, be glory for me!

~ Chas. H. Gabriel (1900)

The felicity, fellowship, fascination, festivity, fun and fabulousness are not the ultimate joy and delight of Heaven. *Heaven's best part is its Host.* It is being in the presence of the One that loved us so much that He paid the supreme price for our salvation, even the death upon an old rugged cross. C. H. Spurgeon, after mentioning many of the glories and wonders of Heaven, said, "But still, for all this, the main thought which we now have of Heaven, and certainly the main fullness of it when we shall come there, is just this: we shall see Jesus."[47] See Revelation 22:4. To behold with sanctified eyes His immaculate glory, beauty and supreme holiness will be "glory for me."

11

8. What Is the Spiritual State of Saints in Heaven?

In Heaven saints will stand faultless before God's throne. Jesus has the authority through His redemptive work at Calvary "to present you faultless before the presence of his glory with exceeding joy" (Jude 24). *Faultless* is a Greek word to describe sacrificial animals without blemish—that which made them fit to be an offering to God.[48] See Exodus 29:1 and Numbers 6:14. We will be *fit* to be in the presence of a thrice holy God by the justifying grace of Jesus.

We presently are not faultless. The old Adamic nature yet trips us up, causing dishonor and reproach to our Savior. At best we are wretched sinners deserving not His mercies but His wrath, not Heaven but Hell. Yea, with Paul we attest, 'I am the chief of sinners' (1 Timothy 1:15). Knowing this and then realizing that a glorious day is coming when we shall stand *faultless* in the King's presence, "rejoicing with exceeding joy," blows me away! This is truly mind-boggling, astonishing and amazing!

Matthew Henry comments, "When believers shall be presented faultless, it will be with exceeding joy. Alas! now our faults fill us with fears, doubts, and sorrows. But *be of good cheer;*…we shall be *presented faultless;* where there is no sin there will be no sorrow; where there is the perfection of holiness, there will be the perfection of joy."[49]

When He shall come with trumpet sound,
Oh, may I then in Him be found
Dressed in His righteousness alone,
Faultless to stand before the throne.
~ Edward Mote (1797–1874)

C. H. Spurgeon summarizes the saint's faultlessness in Heaven: "We shall be unblameable and unreprovable even in His eyes. His law will not only have no charge against us, but it will be magnified in us. Moreover, the work of the Holy Spirit within us will be altogether complete. *He will make us so perfectly holy that we shall have no lingering tendency to sin.* Judgment, memory, will—every power and passion shall be emancipated from the thralldom [captivity] of evil. We shall be holy even as God is holy, and in His presence we shall dwell forever. Saints will not be out of place in Heaven; their beauty will be as great as that of the place prepared for them. Sin gone, Satan shut out, temptation past forever, and ourselves 'faultless' before God—this will be Heaven indeed!"[50] Can you but *imagine* that day, my fellow traveler to Heaven?

9. What Are the Mansions in Heaven?

In Heaven there are "many mansions" (John 14:2). The Greek word for "mansions" is found only in this text and in John 14:23 and is translated "resting places," "abodes," or "permanent dwelling places."[51]

Charles Simeon states, "Here seems to be an allusion to the temple at Jerusalem: God dwelt there in a more especial manner (1 Kings 8:10–11); around it were chambers for the priests and Levites. Thus in Heaven God dwells and displays His glory (Isaiah 57:15); there also are mansions where His redeemed people 'see him as he is.'"[52]

Heaven was designed to accommodate the innumerable unfallen angels and multitudes (the redeemed of the past, present, and future ages[53]) who would enter its domain. There is no danger of insufficient housing for the ransomed of God, given that John's measurements (Revelation 21:16–17) indicate the city consists of nearly 400 quintillion cubic feet. If half of it is reserved for God and His throne and half of the remaining space is used for streets, this would provide a 20-foot cube room for about 12 quadrillion people—many times more than all who have ever lived on earth, even if all had been saved.

Talk about room! There's no danger of a "No Vacancy" sign being hung at Heaven's gate. F. B. Meyer said, "As age after age has poured in its crowds, still the cry has gone forth, 'There is abundant room! The many mansions are not all tenanted. The orchestra is not full.'"[54]

Jesus' use of the term "mansions" indicates distinct, private accommodations for each of His children.[55] The believer's lodging in Heaven will never need maintenance or replacement, for it is eternally durable and permanent.

10. Will Some Receive Positions in Heaven Greater Than Others?

The disciples were informed by Jesus that they would have a special position in Heaven, sitting on twelve thrones judging the twelve tribes of Israel (Luke 22:29–30). To the man that took his two talents and turned them into four talents (parable of the talents), the master said, "'Well done, good and faithful servant! You have been faithful with a few things; I will put you *in charge of many things*. Come and share your master's happiness!'" (Matthew 25:23 NIV). Abraham has a position in Heaven of greater prominence and authority than that of Lazarus (Luke 16:22–31).

James and John requested a seat at Jesus' right and left hands in Glory (Mark 10:37). To this request Jesus responded, "But to sit on my right hand and on my left hand is not mine to give; but it shall be given to them for whom it is prepared" (Mark 10:40). Jesus affirms that in Heaven we will earn greater responsibilities based upon the work done on earth. Knowing that position in Heaven, not entrance there, is based on good works, we ought to be interested in them.[56] "For the Son of man shall come in the glory of his Father with his angels; and then he shall reward every man according to his works" (Matthew 16:27). Although Jesus can give assurance of

Heaven (2 Timothy 2:12); it is God that determines the Heavenly assignments (Mark 10:40).

> It is no matter where I shall be stationed in Heaven, whether I have a high or a low seat there, but to love and please and glorify God is all. ~ David Brainerd

Jonathan Edwards, in preaching upon this subject, said, "Some are designed to sit in higher places there than others; some are designed to be advanced to higher degrees of honor and glory than others are....Though they are all seats of exceeding honor and blessedness, yet some are more so than others."[57] The place and position prepared for the Apostle John certainly is different from that prepared for the dying thief on the Cross. The places and positions prepared for D. L. Moody, Billy Graham, John Wesley and Fanny Crosby are far different from that prepared for Frank Shivers. But *let not your heart be troubled*, the place and position Jesus has prepared for you will be far better than expected or imagined, suited exactly for you.

With regard to position or status in Heaven, I embrace David Brainerd's view stated on his deathbed to Jonathan Edwards, his biographer. Brainerd said, "I do not go to Heaven to be advanced but to give honor to God. *It is no matter where I shall be stationed in Heaven*, whether I have a high or low seat there, but to love and please and glorify God....My Heaven is to please God and glorify Him and give all to Him and to be wholly devoted to His glory."[58] Amen and amen.

11. Are the Saints' Resurrection Bodies Nonmaterial Bodies?

Regarding the saints' body type in Heaven, Paul writes, "They are buried as natural human bodies, but they will be raised as spiritual bodies. For just as there are natural bodies, there are also spiritual bodies" (1 Corinthians 15:44 NLT). Are the saints' resurrection bodies nonmaterial bodies? "If so, it would imply that

Christ's risen body was nonmaterial. This, however, was not what Paul meant. Rather, descendants of fallen Adam cannot enter God's kingdom unchanged. The 'spiritual body' is a true body—a material body—but a transformed body. The two bodies being contrasted are not 'physical' vs. 'spiritual' but rather 'soul-oriented' vs. 'spirit-oriented.'"[59]

The resurrection body of Jesus is the prototype for those whom He has redeemed (1 Corinthians 15:20, 48–49; Philippians 3:21; 1 John 3:2). In the resurrection body, He walked, talked, ate and was recognized (John 21:1–14). Jesus even dismissed the idea that saints in the afterlife would be "disembodied spirits" (Luke 24:37–39). It was "touchable," therefore "feelable" (John 20:27). "It was the same body, yet it was also a different body. The resurrection body retains the personal identity and individuality of the believer, but it will be suited to a new way of life."[60] We will not lose our distinctions as men and women.[61]

> The resurrection body retains the personal identity and individuality of the believer, but it will be suited to a new way of life. ~ Warren Wiersbe

John MacArthur comments, "Adam's body was the prototype of the natural, Christ's body of the resurrection. We will bear the image of His body fit for Heaven (Acts 1:11; Philippians 3:20, 21; 1 John 3:1–3) as we have borne the image of Adam's on earth."[62] Jon Courson elucidates, "Our present bodies of flesh and blood cannot move into the Kingdom because they're not designed for Heaven. That is what death is all about. For the believer, death is simply a way of leaving our earthly tabernacles and moving into our new bodies, exchanging our crusty brown bulbs for creations of beauty."[63]

The saint's spirit immediately at death enters the presence of the Lord; later, at the rapture of the church, it will be reunited with its body, which will be transformed into a glorified body likened to that of Christ (1 Thessalonians 4:16; 1 John 3:2; 1 Corinthians

15:53). "In our resurrection bodies," states Billy Graham, "we will know nothing of physical weakness. Limitations imposed on us on this earth are not known in Heaven. We will have a habitation from God that is incorruptible, immortal, and powerful."[64] Being immortal bodies, they will not decay or die but remain constantly the same.

12. Why Didn't Mary Magdalene Recognize the Risen Jesus?

Mary Magdalene, at the empty tomb of Jesus, failed to recognize Jesus (John 20:11–18). Why?

Commentators vary on an answer to the question—and justly so, for the reason for her not knowing Jesus is not explicitly stated in Scripture. Did she fail to recognize Him due to her great grief and weeping? (The tears didn't prevent her from seeing the two angels or the empty tomb—John 20:11.) Was she simply consumed with all that transpired on the preceding Friday when Jesus was tormented and crucified? Could it have been she wasn't looking to see Jesus, that she didn't anticipate His resurrection, so in her unbelief she didn't "know" Him? Or was it the "glorified body" of Jesus that prevented the instant recognition?

A possible and likely reason for Mary's momentary inability to recognize Jesus could be that her eyes were "holden" *supernaturally* for reasons only known to Jesus, as was the case with the two disciples on the Emmaus Road. See Luke 24:16. The same may be true with regard to the disciples' encounter with the risen Christ at the Sea of Galilee.

But let me be clear that the answer is an unknown. What is known is this. The moment Jesus called Mary's name, she immediately knew Him to be the Lord (John 20:16)! Second, based on the whole of Scripture, His glorified body was not so different from His physical body that it would have been unrecognizable. See Luke 24:39; Matthew 28:9; 1 John 3:2. In each case cited where people, for whatever reason, did not immediately recognize the risen Jesus, they ultimately did.

13. Did Nobody Recognize Jesus in His Glorified Body?

No. It is wrong to say that nobody recognized Jesus in His glorified body. Many did. The Bible says in Matthew 28:9, "And as they went to tell his disciples, behold, Jesus met them, saying, All hail. And they came and held him by the feet, and worshipped him." See Matthew 28:17. To me, a satisfiable explanation for why Mary Magdalene, the two men on the Emmaus Road, and the disciples at the Sea of Galilee did not immediately recognize the risen Christ is cited in Question 12, and evidence that His glorified body was recognizable is cited in Question 14.

14. Was Jesus' Resurrection Body Essentially the Same?

Knowledge about Jesus' glorified body is important to the study of Heaven, for it reveals the kind of body saints will possess in their glorified state. Philippians 3:20–21 states, "But we are citizens of Heaven; our outlook goes beyond this world to the hopeful expectation of the Savior who will come from Heaven, the Lord Jesus Christ. He will remake these wretched bodies of ours to *resemble His own glorious body*, by that power of His which makes Him the master of everything that is" (PHILLIPS).

Was the glorified body of Jesus *like* His physical body? Scripture gives reason to believe that the answer to the question is that it was. In speaking to the disciples, the resurrected Christ said, "Behold my hands and my feet, that it is I myself: handle me, and see; for a spirit hath not flesh and bones, as ye see me have" (Luke 24:39). Later, Jesus shared a meal with them (Luke 24:42–43). The fact that Jesus' glorified body is likened to the physical body He had on the cross is also cited in Peter's witness to Cornelius. He said, "Yet, on the third day, God raised Jesus to life and caused him to be seen, not by all the people, but only by the witnesses God had already chosen. And we are those witnesses *who ate and drank with him after he was raised* from the dead" (Acts 10:40–41 NCV).

But probably the clearest evidence that Jesus' glorified body was *like* His physical body is seen in His encounter with "doubting Thomas." John, recounting the story, says, "The other disciples therefore said unto him (Thomas), We have seen the Lord. But he said unto them, Except I shall see in his hands the print of the nails, and put my finger into the print of the nails, and thrust my hand into his side, I will not believe. And after eight days again his disciples were within, and Thomas with them: then came Jesus, the doors being shut, and stood in the midst, and said, Peace be unto you. Then saith he to Thomas, Reach hither thy finger, and behold my hands; and reach hither thy hand, and thrust it into my side: and be not faithless, but believing" (John 20:25–27). Thomas, convinced it was Jesus, "said unto him, My Lord and my God" (John 20:28).

The key word to understanding the difference between the physical and glorified body of Jesus, and therefore those of the saints, is found in the word *like* (resemble). The one will be *like* the other, but different. "Jesus was distinctly recognizable after His resurrection, and doubtless each individual will have his or her own individual physical identity in eternity."[65]

Spurgeon states, "There was a glorious change, no doubt, in the face of our Lord when it was seen by various brethren after the resurrection. *It was the same face, and they knew Him to be the same Christ.* Did they not put their fingers into the nail prints and thrust their hand into His side? Did they not know Him to be veritable flesh and bone as they saw Him eat the piece of fish and a honeycomb? But the face was restored to its former majesty and radiance."[66]

15. What Makes a Person Afraid to Die?

"Are you afraid?" asked a minister to one of his seriously ill church members. The man was at the point of death and beyond any further medical help. "I've never been afraid of anything in my life," he replied. He then looked at the minister with tears flowing from his eyes and said, "For the first time in my life, I'm terrified— I'm afraid to die."

Upon their dying bed, most identify with the man. Death can be and often is a terrifying experience for any of five reasons.

Death is feared because of the uncertainty of what's beyond the grave, the unknown. It is feared because it means separation from spouse, children and friends. It is feared because of the future judgment that awaits. It is feared because of the process of dying it involves. It is feared because ultimately it is something man faces alone.

> My heart is sore pained within me: and the terrors of death are fallen upon me. ~ Psalm 55:4

What is the antidote to man's fear of dying and death? It is a personal relationship with Jesus Christ through faith and repentance (Acts 20:21). He alone can still *death's* terrorizing, paralyzing and horrifying billows of waves white-capping into the vessel of your life. Luke records the story of the storm-tossed vessel of the disciples on the Sea of Galilee in which their lives were jeopardized (they were fearful of death). Upon their cry for help, Jesus immediately "arose, and rebuked the wind and the raging of the water: and they ceased, and there was a calm" (Luke 8:24). At once the boisterous wind and raging waves became as a sheet of glass.

The "wind and waves" of death outmatch human strength (as the fierce storm outmatched the disciples). Our fortunes, status, abilities, religiosity, intellect or friends are totally inapt to thwart its terrifying waves and frightening noises. But Jesus can and will, upon the soul's request. See John 14:27.

16. Will Saints Be Isolated from Others in Their Various Mansions?

Jesus says Heaven is "my Father's House, indicating its residents will be part of the family of God, and families have unrestricted access one to another. We will not live in isolation. Alexander McLaren says, "A solitary Heaven would be but half a Heaven and would ill correspond with the hopes that inevitably spring from the representation of it as "my Father's house."[67]

17. Will We Have Memories of People Not in Heaven?

The saint's dwarfed perspective now cannot envision Heaven being an awesome place without current family and friends being there. But that will change when we are clothed with an incorruptible body, being transformed into the likeness of Jesus, and gain a heavenly perspective (view things through the lenses of the Lord). There is no case in Scripture of saints in Heaven experiencing sorrow over someone's being absent.

Perhaps this is made possible through the saint's preoccupation with the glory and majesty of Heaven and worship of God. They simply have forgotten this world because of being entirely consumed with the other.[68] Or it may be brought to pass by God's creation of the new order, a New Heaven and New Earth (Revelation 21:1). Could it be that with the New Creation all that was known prior will be forgotten, including people known? Speculative answers based upon texts taken out of context have wide circulation (see the Preface) and must be dismissed.

What is known is that there will be no more tears or sorrow in that Heavenly city (Revelation 21:4). The only way this could be true is by *God's altering the believer's perspective* (and/or memory) regarding earthly relations and friends that are in Hell. The "how" of this is unknown. Personally, I think it's directly linked to the fact that in Heaven "we shall be like him" (1 John 3:2). Presently God's thoughts are not our thoughts (Isaiah 55:8–9). His ways of justice and judgment and mercy are not fully comprehended.[69] But when we are transformed into His likeness, they will be! And that will dictate our emotions in Heaven.

18. How Can Tears Be Wiped Away in Heaven If There Are None?

The Bible says in Revelation 21:4 that in Heaven God "will wipe away all tears from their eyes." There is no ambiguity. It doesn't mean that there will be weeping (tears) in that Heavenly city. It's simply John's poetic way of saying no tears will be there![70] John MacArthur explains it in this way: "Since *there will never be a tear in Heaven*, nothing will be sad, disappointing, deficient, or wrong."[71]

J. F. Walvoord, conservative commentator, says, "Some have wondered if grief and sorrow will exist for a while in Heaven and then be done away. It is better to understand this passage (Revelation 21:4) as saying that Heaven will have none of the features that so characterize the present earth."[72] "With the departure of death, mourning, crying, and disease also disappear, for all these have been caused by the curse of sin affecting God's creation."[73] Since there is no curse of sin in Heaven (which prompts tears of sorrow), there will be no tears (Revelation 22:3).

The banishment of tears is a promise for the future, not now. But until Heaven, the Holy Spirit will minister to our broken hearts, dispensing "holy comfort," wiping away our tears. See John 14:26. The Psalmist states that God records life's tribulations (trials, trouble, and sorrow) in the book of remembrance and treasures up our tears they induce in His "bottle" (Psalm 56:8). Tears are a language that God understands. Not a one flows down the cheek unnoticed or unremembered or uncollected by Him. He counts every teardrop as a liquid jewel to be treasured. To know that He knows when our hearts are ripped inside out over the death of a loved one and He walks with us through that valley of tears makes it bearable. See Question 24, "Is There Cause for Sorrow in Heaven?"

19. Why Do People in Hell Want Loved Ones to Go to Heaven?

My first soul-winning presentation was made in high school to my best friend whose brother had recently died. He wanted to become a Christian, but there was a huge roadblock—spending eternity apart from his brother who died without the Lord. Once I clarified the nature of Hell and its inhabitants' relationships, joyously he received Christ. A Biblical perspective alters thinking.

C. H. Spurgeon, in the sermon "Heaven and Hell," clarifies what relationships in Hell will be like: "What is it that the lost are doing in Hell? They are 'weeping and gnashing their teeth.' Do you gnash [the grinding of the teeth together as in pain, anguish or anger] your teeth now? You would not do it except you were in pain and agony. Well, in Hell there is always gnashing of teeth. And do you know why? There is one gnashing his teeth at his companion and mutters, 'I was led into Hell by you. You led me astray; you taught me to drink the first time.' And the other gnashes his teeth and says, 'What if I did? You made me worse than I should have been in after times.' There is a child who looks at her mother and says, 'Mother, you trained me up to vice.' And the mother gnashes her teeth again at the child and says, 'I have no pity for you, for you excelled me in it and led me into deeper sin.' Fathers gnash their teeth at their sons, and sons at their fathers. And, methinks, if there are any who will have to gnash their teeth more than others, it will be seducers, when they see those whom they have led from the paths of virtue, and hear them saying, 'Ah! we are glad you are in Hell with us; you deserve it, for you led us here.' Have any of you, tonight, upon your consciences the fact that you have led others to the pit? Oh, may sovereign grace forgive you."[74]

Spurgeon's point is biblical; there is no comradeship in Hell (Matthew 13:50). At times people foolishly say, "If I go to Hell, I will be in good company." Sadly, there is even a song with a title that says just that by the group The Dead South. In reality they will be in "bad company." Experiencing that sordid company in Hell, Dives begged Abraham to make every effort to keep his five brothers out of the tormenting place. He didn't want them there. He didn't want them to experience continual, unceasing suffering and anguish as he was doing. So he begs Abraham to send missionaries to their door or Lazarus back from the dead to win them to Christ before it was too late. See Luke 16:19–31. Certainly had Dives found Hell to be a place of enjoyable companionship with friends and family, he never would have begged Abraham to keep them out (Luke 16:27–28).

Sinners that flippantly treat Hell as a fantasy will awaken to its reality at death. John Bunyan describes Hell in *Bunyan's Dying Sayings*: "Sinners' company are the Devil and his angels, tormented in everlasting fire with a curse. Hell would be a kind of paradise if it were not worse than the worst of this world. As different as grief is from joy, as torment from rest, as terror from peace, so different is the state of sinners from that of saints in the world to come."[75] Inhabitants in Hell beg their family members upon earth not to join them, through sermons, preachers, soul winners, Sunday school teachers and missionaries. If heedless, they will participate in the endless "gnashing of teeth" that Spurgeon depicts.

20. Why Do Most Believe They Will Go to Heaven, Not Hell?

According to a 2007 Gallup poll, sixty-four percent of adult Americans believe in Hell and eighty-one percent believe in Heaven.[76] Nearly eighty percent indicated in the poll they expect to go to Heaven at death.[77] That is, the majority of people, almost everyone, believes in Heaven and expects to go there in the afterlife.[78] This differs greatly from Bible facts.

Jesus says regarding Heaven, "Go in through the narrow door. The door is wide and the road is easy that leads to Hell. Many people are going through that door. But the door is narrow and the road is hard that leads to life that lasts forever. *Few people are finding it*" (Matthew 7:13–14 NLV). Upon saying that, Jesus offered a clarification of what was meant: "Many will say to me in that day, Lord, Lord, have we not prophesied in thy name? and in thy name have we cast out devils? and in thy name done many wonderful works? And then will I profess unto them, I never knew you: depart from me, ye that work iniquity" (Matthew 7:22–23). The "many" that expect entrance to Heaven are fooled and deceived and will spend eternity in Hell.

The deception is couched in a misconception of what is required to gain Heaven. It is not religious works or goodness or religious practice or baptism or Holy Communion. It is a personal relationship with Jesus Christ. Paul states, "He saved us because of his mercy, not because of any good things we did. He saved us through the washing that made us new people. He saved us by making us new through the Holy Spirit. God poured out to us that Holy Spirit fully through Jesus Christ our Savior. We were made right with God by his grace" (Titus 3:5–7 ERV).

21. Prior to Going to Heaven, Are Some People Sent to Purgatory?

Purgatory, according to its proponents, is "a state of gradual preparation of the imperfectly sanctified for admission into Heaven."[79] People in Purgatory experience suffering and pain to be purified and cleansed from sin. "The sufferings of those in purgatory vary tremendously in intensity and duration, depending upon the degree to which the baptized but not fully cleansed Christian has sinned."[80]

Purgatory is an attempt to atone for man's sins apart from the blood of Jesus Christ. This is absolutely counter to Biblical teaching. Paul says in Romans 5:8–9, "But God clearly shows and proves His own love for us, by the fact that while we were still sinners, Christ died for us. Therefore, since we have now been justified [declared free of the guilt of sin] by His blood, [how much more certain is it that] we will be saved from the wrath of God through Him" (AMP). Upon the cross, Jesus said, "It is finished" (John 19:30), meaning the price for man's cleansing and deliverance from sin has once and for all been paid through His atoning work.

Nothing more needs to be done. Nothing more can be done. Man cannot be any more "saved" or "forgiven" than he becomes upon acceptance of Jesus Christ as Lord and Savior. The Bible says, "And we can see that it was while we were powerless to help ourselves that Christ died for sinful men. In human experience it is a rare thing for one man to give his life for another, even if the latter be a good man, though there have been a few who have had the courage to do it. Yet the proof of God's amazing love is this: that it was while we were sinners that Christ died for us. Moreover, if he did that for us while we were sinners, now that we are men justified by the shedding of his blood, what reason have we to fear the wrath of God?" (Romans 5:6–9 PHILLIPS).

Nothing beyond the blood of Jesus Christ is needed to atone for sins and escape from the wrath of God. So, to be clear, there is no Purgatory because such a place or state is not needed.

22. Does God Allow Saints a Glimpse of Heaven at Death's Door?

Scripture records the account of Stephen, the first Christian martyr, who testified while dying, "Look, I see the Heavens opened and Jesus the Messiah standing beside God, at his right hand!"

(Acts 7:56 TLB) Similar experiences are shared by Christianity's greatest saints at death (see Question 78, "What Have Saints Said at Death's Door?"). A major difference between their stories and the many shared today is that these saints immediately died and went to Heaven, not to return (as was the case with Stephen).

One must practice caution and keen discernment in accepting stories about Heavenly revelations. Billy Graham cautions us to keep in mind upon hearing such encounters that "Heaven is not a retreat or a place to visit—it is a permanent dwelling."[81] God's only revelation about Heaven and its beauty is in the Holy Bible, not in personal out-of-body experiences.

John MacArthur states there's absolutely no way to gain a better understanding of Heaven than from the pages of Holy Scripture—especially not from dreams or near-death experiences.[82] C. H. Spurgeon agrees, saying, "It's a little Heaven below, to imagine sweet things. But never think that imagination can picture Heaven. When it is most sublime, when it is freest from the dust of earth, when it is carried up by the greatest knowledge and kept steady by the most extreme caution, imagination cannot picture Heaven. 'It hath not entered the heart of man, the things which God hath prepared for them that love him.' Imagination is good, but not to picture to us Heaven. Your imaginary Heaven you will find by-and-by to be all a mistake; though you may have piled up fine castles, you will find them to be castles in the air, and they will vanish like thin clouds before the gale, for imagination cannot make a Heaven. 'Eye hath not seen, nor ear heard, neither hath it entered the heart of man to conceive' it."[83]

> What God revealed in Scripture is the only legitimate place to get a clear understanding of the Heavenly kingdom. ~ John MacArthur

"What God revealed in Scripture," states John MacArthur, "is the only legitimate place to get a clear understanding of the Heavenly kingdom."[84] Billy Graham, addressing the subject emphatically, says, "Our hope must be built on Christ alone and on the promises God has given us in His Word."[85]

23. What Will We Do in Heaven?

"Heaven," declared Ian Maclaren, "is not a Trappist [Trappist monks are known for their strict rule of silence] monastery. Neither is it retirement on pension. No, it is a land of continual progress."[86] Matthew Henry says, "The future glory of the saints will be so entirely different from what they ever knew before that it may well be called new Heavens and a new earth" (2 Peter 3:13).[87] "Behold, I make all things new" (Revelation 21:5). Chuck Swindoll remarks, "What is Heaven like? Playing harps all day? Lounging around on Cloud Nine? Living in enormous mansions along solid gold streets? Does it mean we'll all have long white robes with matching sandals, glowing halos, and big flapping wings? Hardly!"[88]

> Heaven is not a Trappist monastery. Neither is it retirement on pension. No, it is a land of continual progress. ~ Ian Maclaren

So, what will we do in Heaven? W. A. Criswell says, "We shall not be passive spectators, just observing; but we shall be an active, vital part of the whole re-created kingdom of God."[89] W. W. Westcott comments, "We make a great mistake if we connect with our conception of Heaven the thought of rest from work. Rest from toil, from weariness, from exhaustion—yes; rest from work, from productiveness, from service—no. 'They serve God day and night.'"[90]

Saints will *serve* God day and night (Revelation 7:15). Christians who do not delight in that now are in for a big change in Heaven. "There'll be no idleness in Heaven. We will serve Him with perfect joy and happiness."[91] This service implies judging and ruling the world with God (Luke 19:17–19; 1 Corinthians 6:2–3; Jude 14–15). Here we serve Him with frailty, there without limitation or imperfection. "We each shall have a service to render according to how God has made us and endowed us. As we differ in tastes, likes, looks, choices, and abilities, so also we shall differ in our separate assignments and activities."[92]

Saints will *sing* in Heaven (Revelation 5:9). The song of the redeemed in Heaven is: "Worthy is the Lamb that was slain to receive power, and riches, and wisdom, and strength, and honour, and glory, and blessing" (Revelation 5:12). Heaven is a place of endless adoration (worship) of the Lord. The unending praise is fueled by the bountiful mercy of God that makes Heaven possible to the saint. (But were it not for His mercy, we would yet be lost and unfit for Heaven.)

A. W. Tozer comments, "When through the blood of the everlasting covenant we children of the shadows reach at last our Home in the light, we shall have a thousand strings to our harps, but the sweetest may well be the one tuned to sound forth most perfectly the mercy of God."[93] In Heaven, Matthew Henry says, "prayers will there be swallowed up in everlasting praises; there will be no intermission in praising God, and yet no weariness— hallelujahs forever repeated, and yet still new songs. *Hallelujah is the word there* (Revelation 19:1, 3); let us echo to it now, as those that hope to join in it shortly. Hallelujah, praise you the Lord."[94]

> I heard about a mansion
> He has built for me in glory,
> And I heard about the streets of gold
> Beyond the crystal sea,
> About the angels singing
> And the old redemption story,
> And some sweet day I'll sing up there
> The song of victory. ~ Eugene Bartlett (1939)

Saints will *shout* in Heaven. John, in his vision of Heaven, said, "Then I heard again what sounded *like the shouting of a huge crowd*, or like the waves of a hundred oceans crashing on the shore, or like the mighty rolling of great thunder, 'Praise the Lord. For the Lord our God, the Almighty, reigns'" (Revelation 19:6 TLB). If instructed to shout in worship now, certainly it will happen in Heaven once at the majestic throne of our King of Kings! The psalmist gives such directions: "O clap your hands, all ye people; shout unto God with the voice of triumph" (47:1).

I'm gonna shout all over Heaven; what a day that's gonna be.
I'm gonna sing (sing, sing). I'll sing the bass; we'll sing the harmony.
I'll dance right down the streets of gold on Glory Avenue,
And I'll clap my hands and praise the Lord and shout all over Heaven.
~ Legacy Five

Saints will *socialize* in Heaven. Friends of earth will be friends in Heaven. But also think of the fellowship afforded with all the saints of all the ages, including the disciples, evangelists, missionaries, and pastors.

"I cannot think what we shall find to do in Heaven," mused Martin Luther.

"Yes," said Melanchthon, "'Lord, show us the Father, and it sufficeth us.'"

"Why, of course," responded Luther, "that sight will give us quite enough to do!"[95]

24. Is There Cause for Sorrow in Heaven?

"What Heaven holds is no more a reason for rejoicing than what it lacks."[96] Saints in Heaven are healthy and happy, freed from the grip of pain, sickness, crippling illness, suffering, and the constant pull of Satan toward sin (Revelation 21:4). The unpleasant and painful things of this life are vanquished (Revelation 22:3).

The voice of weeping shall be no more heard in her (Isaiah 65:19). Though the text is prophetic regarding the Millennial reign of Christ, it certainly pictures Heaven, where all tears shall be wiped away (Revelation 21:4).

> There will be no tears of misfortune, tears over lost love, tears of remorse, tears of regret, tears over the death of loved ones, or tears for any other reason. ~ John MacArthur

John MacArthur further elucidates, "The first change from their earthly life believers in Heaven will experience is that God will wipe away every tear from their eyes (Revelation 7:17; Isaiah 25:8). That does not mean that people who arrive in Heaven will be crying and God will comfort them. They will not, as some imagine, be weeping as they face the record of their sins. There is no such record. What it declares is the absence of anything to be sorry about—no sadness, no disappointment, no pain. There will be no tears of misfortune, tears over lost love, tears of remorse, tears of regret, tears over the death of loved ones, or tears for any other reason."[97] See Question 18, "How Can Tears Be Wiped Away in Heaven If There Are None?"

In Heaven the saint experiences complete freedom from all that plagued him on earth—evil, suffering, death, sickness, sorrow, sin and Satan. Though conversion and consecration to Christ and the church mitigates such experiences and tremendously eases their load, they cannot ultimately remove them. Why? The world at its core is evil and antagonistic to God and man.[98] The devoted believer is far freer than the carnal saint and the unsaved, yet will not experience perfect, complete freedom until he reaches the shores of Heaven. "The believer's rebirth through faith in Christ brings newness to that person's life, but it is only in the eternal state that God will make all things new."[99] See 2 Corinthians 5:17.

Saints join with all creation in groaning and longing for deliverance from earth's sufferings, diseases, sicknesses, afflictions and struggles. Paul writes, "For we know that all creation has been groaning as in the pains of childbirth right up to the present time.

And we believers also groan, even though we have the Holy Spirit within us as a foretaste of future glory, for we long for our bodies to be released from sin and suffering. We, too, wait with eager hope for the day when God will give us our full rights as his adopted children, including the new bodies he has promised us" (Romans 8:22–23 NLT).

Until the time of our departure to Heaven, we must faithfully and earnestly engage in warfare against evil and the evil one to retain what freedom is possessed. See Ephesians 6:11–13.

> After the midnight, morning will greet us;
> After the sadness, joy will appear.
> After the tempest, sunlight will meet us;
> After the jeering, praise we shall hear.
>
> After the battle, peace will be given;
> After the weeping, song there will be.
> After the journey, there will be Heaven;
> Burdens will fall, and we shall be free.
>
> Shadows and sunshine all thro' the story,
> Teardrops and pleasure, day after day,
> But when we reach the Kingdom of Glory,
> Trials of earth will vanish away. ~ James Rowe (1915)

25. In Heaven Will There Be Time?

Will Heaven be the *perpetual present*? Advocates of this view generally base their reasoning on Heaven's being an abode where the sun does not shine by day or the moon by night (Revelation 21:23–25). Measurement of time on earth is based upon both the sun and the moon. However, in the *New Jerusalem* (Heaven), that standard of measurement is unnecessary.

Scripture does reference time in Heaven in several places. In Revelation 8:1, John says, "When the Lamb broke the seventh seal on the scroll, there was silence throughout Heaven for about *half an hour*" (NLT). In Revelation 6:10–11, the martyred saints in Heaven ask of God *how much longer* it would be before their murderers were judged and punished. In response to the prayer they were given white robes and instructed to *"rest yet for a little season."* In Revelation 22:1–2, John pictures the tree of life with its twelve kinds of fruits *bearing fruit each month*. Peter informs us "that one day is with the Lord as a thousand years, and a thousand years as one day" (2 Peter 3:8). God is not bound by time, for He exists apart from it. But whether the same is true for glorified saints is an unknown.

All that may be said is that it appears time will exist in Heaven but its nature or composition is not revealed. Whatever its substance, it will not in the least interfere with the saints' glorious fellowship with the family of God, work and worship. And it certainly will not jeopardize the saints' rest, for in that Heavenly city they will be in a perpetual state of rest, for they worship the Lord and do His assigned work "day and night" (Revelation 14:13; 7:15).

If glorified saints experience time the same way God does (a thousand years as a day) that means our family members and friends haven't been there an hour yet!

26. Are There Baptists, Methodists and Presbyterians in Heaven?

John Wesley dreamed that he died and stood before the gatekeeper of Heaven. Anxious as to who might have been admitted, he made inquiry of the gatekeeper.

"Are there any Presbyterians here?"

"None," replied the keeper of the gate.

Wesley was surprised. "Have you any Anglicans?" he asked.

"Not one!" was the reply.

"Surely there must be many Baptists in Heaven."

"No, none," replied the keeper.

Wesley grew pale. He was afraid to ask his next question: "How many Methodists are there in Heaven?"

"Not one," answered the keeper quickly.

Wesley was then told that in Heaven there were no earthly distinctions like denominations. "All of us here in Heaven are one in Christ. We are just an assembly who love the Lord."

Though it was but a dream, it nonetheless spoke truth. Denominations are of man's invention; the church is God's creation (Matthew 16:18–20; Colossians 1:18; 1 Peter 2:6). In Heaven there will be no denominational tags of any kind, only people that are washed in the blood of Jesus. Disunity and division known among saints in the "church" on earth will be nonexistent in Heaven. The high priestly prayer of Jesus for His church will be realized: "That they may be one, as we are" (John 17:11).

Jesus instituted the church and stated that it is His body, that He is its head and chief cornerstone, that it's His house ("My house") and that it "shall be called the house of prayer" (Matthew 21:13). Identification with and involvement in His church is important. We are cautioned not to forsake the church (Hebrews 10:25). It is essential for spiritual growth and corporate worship with fellow believers. Pray for it, give to it, serve through it, attend it and worship at it, but never rely upon it as the basis for eternal life in Heaven.

27. Is Anyone Too Evil to Go to Heaven?

Scripture gives a clear and definitive answer in 1 Corinthians 6:9–11: "Have you forgotten that the kingdom of God will never belong to the wicked? Don't be under any illusion—neither the impure, the idolater or the adulterer; neither the effeminate, the pervert or the thief; neither the swindler, the drunkard, the foul-mouthed or the rapacious shall have any share in the kingdom of God. And such men, remember, were some of you! But you have cleansed yourselves from all that, you have been made whole in spirit, you have been justified before God in the name of the Lord Jesus and in his very Spirit" (PHILLIPS).

The worst of sinners cannot gain Heaven any more than the least of sinners can. But all sinners, regardless of degree of their wicked behavior and opposition to God, upon genuine belief and repentance, have a place reserved in Heaven. Note that Paul indicated specifically that some of the saints at Corinth were among the most wicked of society until their conversion, at which point they became heirs of the Kingdom of God in Heaven. And as for himself, it is stated that he sanctioned the murder of Stephen, the first Christian martyr (Acts 22:20). Yet Jesus saved him miraculously and gave him a place in Heaven.

The Bible says, "For whosoever shall call upon the name of the Lord shall be saved" (Romans 10:13). Note the "whosoever" is not qualified; therefore, it references anybody and everybody, regardless of conduct—even you.

28. What Can the Saint Do to Keep Heaven on His Mind?

During the time of exile from Jerusalem (the holy city), the psalmist, in behalf of all the Israelites, said, "If I forget you, O Jerusalem, let my right hand forget its skill upon the harp. If I fail to love her more than my highest joy, let me never sing again" (Psalm 137:5–6 TLB). The Israelites refused to allow their persecution or the allurements of Babylon to erase the memory of the holy city, Jerusalem. They forthrightly fixed their thoughts and affections upon the city and were willing to be deprived of their ability to play the harp or to sing (or do either rightly) should Jerusalem cease to be their highest joy (crown of all joys).[100]

There is great spiritual implication of the text as it relates to the believer. The saint is in exile (Babylon, type of the evil world) under great oppression and persecution orchestrated by Satan. He, like the Israelites, is to constantly remember the glory and beauty of Zion (but his is Heaven, the eternal Zion) and long for it. So intense ought to be the saints' fixation on Heaven that they refuse to allow the allurements or adversities of the world to blur its reality or eclipse its wondrous benefits and glorious fellowship with God and the family of God or silence their voices in joyous song.

Believers must remember that they are in spiritual exile, that their homeland is Zion (the New Jerusalem, Heaven). "For our conversation [citizenship] is in Heaven; from whence also we look for the Savior, the Lord Jesus Christ" (Philippians 3:20). See Hebrews 13:14. The holy saint will never be content or satisfied in the world, for it's antagonistic to God and himself. What he can and must do is refuse to allow the world, through its unrelenting oppression, to suffocate his chief joy (Heaven) and silence his tongue in gleefully talking and singing about Heaven. See Revelation 12:11.

C. S. Lewis wrote, "If you read history, you will find that the Christians who did most for the present world were precisely those who thought most of the next. It is since Christians have largely ceased to think of the other world that they have become so ineffective in this."[101]

29. What Are the Crowns Saints May Obtain in Heaven?

The Greek word translated "crown" is *stephanos* (from which was derived the name of the first Christian martyr, Stephen) which means "crown, wreath." A crown was literally worn around the head of victors in athletic contests in Paul's day as an award.

Paul references the crown in several passages, including 1 Corinthians and 2 Timothy, relating it to the believer. He states, "All athletes are disciplined in their training. They do it to win a *prize* [crown, wreath] that will fade away, but we do it for an eternal *prize* [crown, wreath]" (1 Corinthians 9:25 NLT), and "An athlete is not *crowned* unless he competes according to the rules" (2 Timothy 2:5 ESV). Further, Paul personally fully expected to receive a crown in Heaven, for he says, "Now, a crown is being held for me—a crown for being right with God. The Lord, the judge who judges rightly, will give the crown to me on that day—not only to me but to all those who have waited with love for him to come again" (2 Timothy 4:8 NCV).

The Bible reveals five Heavenly crowns the believer may receive in Heaven.

The Imperishable Crown. "You know that only one person gets a crown for being in a race even if many people run. You must run so you will win the crown. Everyone who runs in a race does many things so his body will be strong. He does it to get a crown that will soon be worth nothing, but we work for a crown that will last forever" (1 Corinthians 9:24–25 NLV). The imperishable or incorruptible crown is for the believer who, like an athlete, disciplines the body into subjection to Christ and becomes victorious over the flesh and who faithfully runs the Christian race to the finish line (faithful endurance, perseverance).

The Crown of Rejoicing. "You are our hope, our joy, and the crown we will take pride in when our Lord Jesus Christ comes" (1 Thessalonians 2:19 NCV). Paul regarded the Thessalonians whom he won through soul winning and preaching as his crown. Theologians often refer to this crown as *the crown of soul winning*. Saints that win souls to Christ will be the recipients of this crown. Paul anticipated seeing his "trophies of grace" (converts to Christ) in Heaven and declared that would be a great delight and joy. Ponder the thought and the joy that will be yours in Heaven in seeing your "trophies of grace." Certainly it will be shouting time in Heaven when you do. Amen! See Daniel 12:3.

The Crown of Life. "Have no fear of what you will suffer. I tell you now that the devil is going to cast some of your number into prison where your faith will be tested and your distress will last for ten days. Be faithful in the face of death and I will give you the crown of life" (Revelation 2:10 PHILLIPS). This crown is for the persecuted saint that endures suffering, and perhaps even death, bravely for the cause of Christ.

The Crown of Righteousness. "And now the prize awaits me— the crown of righteousness, which the Lord, the righteous Judge, will give me on the day of his return. And the prize is not just for me but for all who eagerly look forward to his appearing" (2 Timothy 4:8 NLT). This wondrous crown will be given to believers who look with anticipation for Jesus' return.

The Crown of Glory. "And when the chief Shepherd shall appear, ye shall receive a crown of glory that fadeth not away" (1 Peter 5:4). This may be called *the pastor's crown.* It is given to pastors who faithfully proclaim Christ, feed the flock of God, exhibit spiritual oversight for the flock of God, and lead by worthy example. "Henceforth there is laid up for me a crown of righteousness, which the Lord, the righteous judge, shall give me at that day: and not to me only, but unto all them also that love (or, have loved) His appearing" (2 Timothy 4:8). No believer will be crowned until Paul receives the crown of righteousness as his reward "at that day"—the day of Christ.[102] He says, "Behold, I come quickly; and my reward is with me, to give every man according as his work shall be" (Revelation 22:12). Jesus clearly states that no rewards will be given until the rapture of the saints. Thus, it follows there will be no crowned elders until after the rapture.[103]

The race will soon be finished, and then following the rapture, provided you have faithfully endured to the end, the King of Glory will place upon your head the victor's crown(s) you have *won.* Keep focusing on the finish line. Strain every spiritual muscle to compete well and finish strong. Strive to obtain every crown that may be gained. Say with Paul, "I strain to reach the end of the race and receive the prize for which God is calling us up to Heaven because of what Christ Jesus did for us" (Philippians 3:14 TLB).

30. What Will the Saints in Heaven Do with Their Crowns?

John, in the vision of Heaven given him by Jesus, sees, "The four and twenty elders fall down before him that sat on the throne, and worship him that liveth for ever and ever, and cast their crowns before the throne, saying, Thou art worthy, O Lord, to receive glory and honor and power: for thou hast created all things, and for thy pleasure they are and were created" (Revelation 4:10–11).

The elders are the representatives of all the redeemed who have died in the past or who shall be living at the Lord's return.[104] "They cast their crowns," states Matthew Henry, "before the throne; they gave God the glory of the holiness wherewith He had crowned their souls on earth and the honor and happiness with which He crowns them in Heaven. They owe all their graces and all their glories to Him, and acknowledge that His crown is infinitely more glorious than theirs, and that it is their glory to be glorifying God."[105]

The *casting of crowns* was practiced in the East by petty kings to show honor, respect, and submission to the supremacy of the emperor.[106] An example of this practice is seen in Tiridates' laying his crown before the image of Nero as a token of his homage.[107]

Saints will with deep humility, honor, adoration and submission cast their crowns at Jesus' feet in acknowledgement that all merit for them is due to Him[108] and as a gift (as meager as it is in comparison to all He has done in their behalf) of utter gratitude for His, and thus their, utter triumph over Satan and the demons of Hell.

31. Might My Name Be Stricken from the Book of Life?

At the moment a person experiences the new birth (born-again) his or her name is written with *indelible ink* in the Lamb's Book of Life (Heaven's registry of its citizens). See Philippians 4:3. Only people that have their names written in that Book may enter Heaven's pearly gates. John says, "Nothing sinful will go into the city. No one who is sinful-minded or tells lies can go in. Only those whose names are written in the Lamb's book of life can go in" (Revelation 21:27 NLV). See Revelation 20:12, 15.

To all who have their names recorded in the Book of Life, Jesus promises nothing will remove it. He says, "I will never blot his name out of the book of life. I will confess his name before my Father and before his angels" (Revelation 3:5 ESV).

H. A. Ironside, in *Eternal Security of the Believer,* wrote, "When we speak of the eternal security of the believer, what do we mean? We mean that once a poor sinner has been regenerated by the Word and the Spirit of God, once he has received a new life and a new nature and has been made partaker of the divine nature, once he has been justified from every charge before the throne of God, it is absolutely impossible that that man should ever again be a lost soul."[109]

It must be underscored that the criterion for eternal security (name never blotted out of the Book of Life) is not mere religious profession, practice or piety. Jesus cautioned about being religious without being redeemed. He said, "When the Judgment Day comes, many will say to me, 'Lord, Lord! In your name we spoke God's message, by your name we drove out many demons and performed many miracles!' Then I will say to them, 'I never knew you. Get away from me, you wicked people!'" (Matthew 7:22–23 GNT).

One may preach like Nicodemus, be devoted to the church like Saul of Tarsus, be baptized like Simon Magus, and be a respected and trusted officer among the saints (church) like Judas (disciple band)

and miss Heaven. To such as these that are religious but not reborn, Jesus will say at the Judgment, "I never knew you." Note that He does not say to them, "I knew you but now I don't. Your name was written in the Book of Life, but now I've blotted it out." He says, "I *never* knew you."

> We do not pretend to give certificates of salvation, and if we did they would be worthless; you must yourselves know the Lord and be really converted, or else your profession is a forgery and you yourselves are counterfeits. ~ C.H. Spurgeon

C. H. Spurgeon cautions, "We do not pretend to give certificates of salvation, and if we did they would be worthless; you must yourselves know the Lord and be really converted, or else your profession is a forgery and you yourselves are counterfeits."[110]

Make certain of salvation; then rest assured that your name will never, never, never be blotted out of God's record book of the redeemed.

32. Is Heaven a Reward for a Good Life?

Barna research reveals a disheartening statistic about evangelical Christians with regard to belief about the means of obtaining Heaven. They report, "Many committed born-again Christians believe that people have multiple options for gaining entry to Heaven. They are saying, in essence, 'Personally, I am trusting Jesus Christ as my means of gaining God's permanent favor and a place in Heaven—but someone else could get to Heaven based upon living an exemplary life.'"[111]

Are they correct? Can a person in fact gain Heaven by living a clean and moral upstanding life? or by being religious-minded and God-fearing? or by being baptized, confirmed, christened, and/or serving others through the church? Lest you misunderstand me because you read no further, it must be stated clearly and forthrightly that such a view is doctrinally flawed and therefore absolutely wrong.

The Scripture clearly teaches that man's salvation (means of abundant life now and Heaven hereafter) is not based upon good works or moral living but rather the personal relationship with Jesus Christ through the new birth (John 3:3). Paul states, "Then he [Jesus] saved us—not because we were good enough to be saved but because of his kindness and pity—by washing away our sins" (Titus 3:5). The truth is presented again and again in biblical texts such as Ephesians 2:8–9; Romans 10:3; Colossians 2:18–23; Romans 4:4–5; Romans 6:23; Romans 9:16; Romans 11:6 and Galatians 2:16.

> The Scripture clearly teaches that man's salvation (means of abundant life now and Heaven hereafter) is not based upon good works or moral living but rather the personal relationship with Jesus Christ through the new birth (John 3:3).

These passages and the whole of Scripture make it crystal clear that obedience to the Ten Commandments or morality or man's works has nothing to do with salvation. It is a totally free gift of God to everyone that believeth. Salvation is a *gift* to be received, not a *reward* to be earned. Christianity isn't a list of things to do. It is a relationship made possible through what Christ has done for man on the cross. Man is saved by Jesus' work, not his own. This fact alone differentiates Christianity from the religions of the world.

In the sermon *Faith in Perfection,* C. H. Spurgeon said, "If there is one stitch in the celestial garment of my righteousness which I am to insert myself, then I am lost. If there is one drachma [a coin] in the price of my redemption which I am to make up, then I must perish. If there is one contingency—one 'if' or 'though' or 'but' about my soul's salvation—then I am a lost man."[112] Spurgeon's point is obvious, is it not? The only means by which sinful man may get right with holy God and gain Heaven is not through human effort but through repentance over sin (expression of earnest sorrow over wrongdoing) and placement of faith (trustful acceptance) in the Lord Jesus Christ as Lord and Savior (Acts 20:21).

The "way" to Heaven is by being born again (John 3:3). Man's present nature is defiled and corrupt to the core, totally unfit to enter the presence of Holy God in Heaven. He must have a new (divine) nature. This nature (opposite of the former) is implanted within man at the moment of the new birth (2 Peter 1:4), making Heaven possible. How is a man born again? How does he receive the divine nature?

Jesus gives answer in His dialog with Nicodemus (John 3). He says to him, "Just as Moses lifted up the [bronze] serpent in the desert [on a pole], so must the Son of Man be lifted up [on the cross], so that whoever believes will in Him have eternal life [after physical death, and will actually live forever]. For God so [greatly] loved and dearly prized the world, that He [even] gave His [One and] only begotten Son, so that whoever believes and trusts in Him [as Savior] shall not perish, but have eternal life" (John 3:14–16 AMP). The Israelites bitten by a venomous snake in the wilderness had only one hope of cure, to look up in faith at a brazen serpent lifted up on a pole. Man has been bitten and smitten by the disease of sin, and his only cure is to look up in faith to Jesus on the cross. See John 3:14–15 and Numbers 21:5–9.

Look and live abundantly, presently, and eternally in Heaven. Jesus completed the conversation with Nicodemus by saying, "For God sent not his Son into the world to condemn the world; but that the world through him might be saved. He that believeth on him is not condemned: but he that believeth not is condemned already, because he hath not believed in the name of the only begotten Son of God" (John 3:17–18).

Come, then, and join this holy band and on to glory go
To dwell in that celestial land where joys immortal flow.
Only trust Him; only trust Him; only trust Him now.
He will save you; He will save you; He will save you now.

~ John H. Stockton (1874)

33. Is Everybody Going to Heaven?

Universalism is the belief that *all* people at death will experience some form of happiness regardless of whether or not they accept Jesus Christ as Savior and Lord. Shockingly, universalism is escalating among Christians.

J. I. Packer states, "Universalism does not stand up to biblical examination. Its sunny optimism may be reassuring and comfortable, but it wholly misses the tragic quality of human sin, human unbelief, and human death set forth in the Bible. Universalism reinvents, and thereby distorts, biblical teaching about God and salvation."[113] O. C. Quick, former professor of theology at Oxford, cites two most explicit Scripture texts that affirm permanent and painful punishment for the unbeliever after death: Matthew 25 and Revelation 20:15. This great scholar stated that the *anti-universalist teaching* in the New Testament is "conclusive."[114]

> The vague and tenuous hope that God is too kind to punish the ungodly has become a deadly opiate for the consciences of millions. ~ A.W. Tozer

Scripture is crystal clear. It leaves absolutely no room for misunderstanding or misinterpretation regarding a personal relationship with Jesus Christ as the *only* means of accessing Heaven at death (John 10:9; John 14:6; Romans 10:9–13). Likewise, it is just as clear with regard to the eternal punishment (Hell) for the unbeliever (Matthew 25:46; Mark 9:48; Luke 16:19–31; Revelation 9:11). "The vague and tenuous hope," says A. W. Tozer, "that God is too kind to punish the ungodly has become a *deadly opiate* for the consciences of millions."[115]

34. At What Moment Do Saints Enter Heaven?

Saints enter Heaven immediately upon death. Paul pointedly states that "to be absent from the body [is] to be present with the Lord" (2 Corinthians 5:8). At the moment that Lazarus died, angels escorted him into the presence of God in Heaven (Luke 16:22). The saint shuts his eyes in death and opens them instantly in Heaven. The epitaph on the tombstone of Solomon Peas, London, England, expresses this biblical truth.

> Beneath these clouds and beneath these trees
> Lies the body of Solomon Peas.
> This is not Peas; it is only his pod.
> Peas has shelled out and gone Home to God.[116]

The only Christians that attend a funeral are those that are alive and well, for any believer who dies is in the presence of the Lord.

Thomas Watson states, "When death shall give the fatal stroke, there shall be an exchange of earth for Heaven, of imperfect enjoyments for perfect enjoyments of God. Then the soul shall be swallowed up with a full enjoyment of God; no corner of the soul shall be left empty, but all shall be filled up with the fullness of God. Here in this present world, they receive grace, but in Heaven they shall receive glory. God keeps the best wine until last; the best of God, Christ, and Heaven is beyond this present world. Here we have but some sips, some tastes of God; fullness is reserved for the glorious state. He who sees most of God here on earth sees but His back parts; His face is a jewel of that splendor and glory which no eye can behold but a glorified eye."[117]

35. What Does Changed in the "Twinkling of an Eye" Mean?

We are told that when Jesus returns to rapture the saints to Heaven, they will be changed "in a moment, in the twinkling of an eye" (1 Corinthians 15:52). What does this mean?

In a moment, in the twinkling of an eye. "When used of time ('moment'), it represents an extremely short unit of time, a flash, an instant, a unit of time that cannot be divided. A second can be

CAUGHT UP TO HEAVEN

calibrated to one-tenth, one one-hundredth, and one one-thousandth of a second. But how do you calibrate an 'atomic' second? Christ's return will be in an 'atomic' second."[118] John MacArthur says the "twinkling of an eye" was "Paul's way of showing how brief the 'moment' will be. The Greek word for 'twinkling' refers to any rapid movement. Since the eye can move more rapidly than any other part of our visible bodies, it seems to well illustrate the sudden transformation of raptured believers."[119]

So when Jesus returns to rapture the saints, the bodies of those alive will be immediately transformed into His likeness (like Jesus' resurrected body), and the dead saints will be raised with new glorified bodies.[120] All of this occurs faster than the *blink* of the eye. Note that saints yet alive will be changed without going through the death process. The quickness of Jesus' coming prevents soul preparation. Now is the time to get ready for His coming and the Judgment.

36. What Do You Say to One Who Doesn't Believe in Heaven?

The question itself underscores the fact the person doesn't believe the Bible to be the divinely inspired, authoritative Word of God, for it speaks of Heaven's reality 582 times. If belief in the Bible was exhibited, then the question would be moot.

Totally true in fact and doctrine, the Bible contains no contradictions and is thoroughly trustworthy. "Through the Holy Spirit's agency, God is involved in both the production and interpretation of Scripture. Men of God in antiquity spoke as they were moved by the Holy Spirit. 'Moved' means literally 'to bear along.' Scripture is infallible precisely because the Holy Spirit 'bore along' the prophets who spoke and wrote."[121] See 2 Peter 1:20–21; 2 Timothy 3:16.

While the Bible validates itself through an array of internal supports of its reliability—consistency, multiple witnesses, verifiable history—the Bible is also validated by many external evidences. For instance, the accuracy of historical events presented in the Bible are supported by 23,000 archaeological digs,[122] and hundreds of fulfilled prophecies provide evidence for its divine inspiration and infallibility. The redeemed also testify to its truthfulness by its eternal impact upon their life.

Ultimately, despite all the indisputable evidence for the Bible, the Holy Spirit must open man's eyes to believe it as true. When a man accepts the Bible as God's Word, then other issues such as the reality of Heaven vanish. Pray that the *eye salve* of illumination regarding the credibility of the Bible be applied by the Holy Spirit to them who are spiritually blinded. See Revelation 3:18.

37. How Do Saints Get to Heaven?

Jesus assures the saints that He personally will escort them into Heaven at His coming (John 14:3). At least one man is known to have been escorted to Heaven by angels upon his death (Luke 16:22). One fact is most certain. God will make sure His children arrive safely in their eternal home. There is absolutely zero chance that a saint will mistakenly wind up in Hell. In light of this truth, there is no reason to fear nor for your heart to be troubled that you will be sent to Hell accidentally (John 14:1).

> There is absolutely zero chance that a saint will mistakenly wind up in Hell.

C. Stanford writes, "Dying may be regarded as a mode in which Christ comes for His people, one by one. Death is not coming; death is not a person, only a door to which Christ, the sovereign Lord who has at His girdle the keys of death and the unseen state, comes."[123]

Regarding death as the conveyance God uses to take us to Heaven, Martyn Lloyd-Jones states, "But let me hasten to add that though Christians are still subject to death, their view of death should be entirely different from that of the unbeliever. Why? Because of what they know. You can see this, for instance, in that great statement in 1 Corinthians 15:55. Every one of us should be able to look in the face of death and say, 'O death, where is thy sting? O grave, where is thy victory?' This does not mean that we speak lightly and loosely and flippantly about death, but it does mean that we know that its sting has been taken away by the atoning death of Christ and by the satisfaction He gave to the law. We know, too, the teaching of the Apostle Paul about death being a 'gain': 'Having a desire to...be with Christ,' he says, 'which is far better' (Philippians 1:21–23), while Revelation 14:13 tells us, 'Blessed are the dead which die in the Lord.'"[124]

It was the peculiar saying of a dying man, who exclaimed: "I have no fear of going home. God's finger is on the latch, and I am ready for Him to open the door. It is but the entrance to my Father's house."[125]

After Charles E. Fuller had announced the sermon subject of "Heaven" for the approaching Sunday, he received a letter from a sickly old gentleman. In part the man wrote:

"Next Sunday you are to talk about Heaven. I am interested in that Land, because I have held a clear title to a bit of property there for over fifty-five years. I did not buy it. It was given to me without money and without price. But the Donor purchased it for me at tremendous sacrifice. I am not holding it for speculation since the title is not transferable. It is not a vacant lot.

"For more than half a century I have been sending materials out of which the greatest Architect and Builder of the Universe has been building a home for me which will never need to be remodeled nor repaired because it will suit me perfectly, individually, and will never grow old.

"Termites can never undermine its foundations, for they rest on the Rock of Ages. Fire cannot destroy it. Floods cannot wash it away. No locks or bolts will ever be placed upon its doors, for no vicious person can ever enter that land where my dwelling stands, now almost completed and almost ready for me to enter in and abide in peace eternally, without fear of being ejected.

"There is a valley of deep shadow between the place where I live in California and that to which I shall journey in a very short time. I cannot reach my home in that City of Gold without passing through this dark valley of shadows. But I am not afraid, because the best Friend I ever had went through the same valley long, long ago and drove away all its gloom. He has stuck by me through thick and thin since we first became acquainted fifty-five years ago, and I hold His promise in printed form never to forsake me or leave me alone. He will be with me as I walk through the valley of shadows, and I shall not lose my way when He is with me.

"I hope to hear your sermon on Heaven next Sunday from my home in Los Angeles, California, but I have no assurance that I shall be able to do so. My ticket to Heaven has no date marked for the journey, no return coupon, and no permit for baggage. Yes, I am all ready to go, and I may not be here while you are talking next Sunday evening, but I shall meet you there someday."[126]

In summary, "It does not satisfy Him [God] to snatch us from destruction, to open Heaven for us, to bring us into the way to it, to make us meet for it; He will come Himself and take us to it. And when we are there, He will not say, 'There is the door of My Father's house open for you; you may now enter in'; He will not leave angels to welcome us, or our holy ministers and friends who have gone before, to receive us; He Himself will come like a parent to His door to receive there His long expected and beloved child."[127] See John 14:3.

38. Do Saints in Heaven Know What's Happening on Earth?

Often Hebrews 12:1 ("cloud of witnesses") is used as a proof text that glorified saints are watching saints on earth from the grandstand of Heaven. But does it teach that as a fact? The text reads, "Therefore, since we are surrounded by such a great cloud of witnesses, let us throw off everything that hinders and the sin that so easily entangles. And let us run with perseverance the race marked out for us" (NIV).

"Wherefore" or "therefore" (reference back to Chapter 11, which cites 18 heroes of the faith) seeing we (saints of earth) also are "compassed about" (encircled about) with so great a "cloud" ("figure of speech indicating a large group"[128]) "of witnesses" (the people of Chapter 11 to whom God gave commendation for their constancy of faith). Kenneth Wuest states, "The word [witnesses] does not include in its meaning the idea of a person *looking at something*."[129] Donald Hagner supports Wuest in stating, "Witnesses here does not mean observers of the present conduct of Christians, but rather those who testify or give evidence of the victorious life of faith."[130]

To summarize, the deceased heroes of the faith of Chapter 11 are those in the Heavenly "grandstand" bearing witness (providing evidence) to saints on earth of the wonderful value and benefit of living by faith.[131] "We are watching them for encouragement rather than them watching us in examination."[132]

It is by the observation of their godly example lived on earth that the saints are encouraged to run the race strenuously, perseveringly, and victoriously. Therefore, when facing gigantic problems, remember David who slew Goliath. In times of tumultuous trials, remember Shadrach, Meshach, and Abed-nego who survived the fiery furnace. Upon embarking upon the unknown in service to God, remember Abraham and be encouraged. In times of false accusations, remember Joseph in Potiphar's jail. And in seasons of affliction and persecution for the Gospel's sake, remember Moses in Pharaoh's house. Remember, and in remembering be encouraged, uplifted, inspired and motivated to press onward in the race regardless of the obstacles

Satan hurls upon you. Let the Heavenly saints cheer you on to the finish line!

So, can saints in Heaven watch us on earth? A trusted name in conservative theology, Warren Wiersbe, says, "This image does not necessarily imply that people in Heaven watch us or know what is going on here on earth. It is an illustration, not a revelation."[133] Whether these heroes actually observe us on earth may be suggested by the text but certainly doesn't conclusively prove it.

The only concrete thing of which we are sure is that glorified saints know when a sinner is saved (Luke 15:7).[134] Whether they witness it firsthand or receive the news by an angel is simply not known. Billy Graham said, "The Bible does not tell us if the souls in God's presence know what is happening on earth. What it does tell us is that God knows what is happening in our lives."[135] And that's far more important and to me totally sufficient.

> The only truth that may be categorically stated is that saints in Heaven have access to knowledge to some degree of world happenings. All else is mere speculation.

Other Biblical Passages on the Subject

From Heaven, Abraham and Lazarus saw the rich man in Hell (Luke 16:23–26). It is plausible to think that if a person in Heaven could see what was happening in Hell, then he likewise could see what was happening on earth, at least to some degree, but this is mere conjecture. Additionally, in the same narrative, the rich man in Hell knows that all five of his brothers are still unsaved (Luke 16:27–28). How did he know? Scripture does not give answer. Samuel's knowledge in Heaven of what was occurring on earth between King Saul and Israel (1 Samuel 28:16–18) supports the view that saints in Heaven will be informed of what transpires on earth to some extent, as does the request of the martyrs in Heaven to know how much longer it would be before their persecutors (murderers) would be punished (Revelation 6:9–10). The only truth that may be categorically stated is that saints in Heaven have access to knowledge to some degree of world happenings. All else is mere conjecture, speculation or theology based on sincere but spurious biblical interpretation. This is one of many "secrets" that will be revealed about Heaven upon arrival. See Deuteronomy 29:29.

39. Do Saints in Heaven Know If Family Members Get Saved?

Saints in Heaven rejoice with the host of Heaven over news of a soul being saved. Whether they are told of the news or they see it happen is unknown (Luke 15:7). So, the answer to the question is a loud yes.

There is much joy in Heaven over one sinner that repents (Luke 15:7). "The implication is that it is joy throughout Heaven, from center to circumference—joy on the throne and joy in those who serve under it; joy in the heart of God and among all the hosts of God; joy for Christ's sake, for the penitent's sake, for Heaven's sake; joy that a broken link has been repaired in the holy creation of God; joy that another precious jewel has been added to the crown of redeeming love; joy that there is born another tenant for the mansions of glory; joy that another symptom has transpired of the ultimate recovery of all the downtrodden fields of creation which sin has overrun."[136] Note they rejoice with *much* or *more* joy, indicating it is possible to have *less* joy in Heaven.

> There's joy in the camp; a sinner has come home.
> There's joy in the camp, rejoicing 'round the throne.
> Singing and shouting the great redemption song,
> There's joy, wondrous joy in the camp. ~ William J. Gaither

Undoubtably, all of Heaven momentarily stops what they are doing to celebrate the salvation of even one sinner. That's how much one soul is valued in Heaven. Do we stop our work or fun and drop to our knees in celebration upon news of someone's getting saved? Get used it, for you will in Heaven.

40. Will Children That Die in Infancy or Prior to the Age of Understanding Enter Heaven?

David said regarding the death of his infant child, "I will go to him one day, but he cannot return to me" (2 Samuel 12:23 NLT). David was certain he would see his son in the eternal abode called Heaven. God included this story in Scripture, knowing that David would not be the only parent who would grieve the loss of a dearly loved child, to grant comfort and assurance of seeing him or her again.

Who can tell whether God will be gracious to me, that the child may live? As long as the child was alive, there was hope God would raise him up. It is proper to pray for the healing of relatives (and others) on sickbeds until either it is known that it is God's will to take them Home (then prayer is for "dying grace") or they are raised up to renewed health. Granted we cannot always know God is taking someone to Heaven; therefore, being uncertain, saints ought to keep praying for the person's deliverance, for 'who can tell whether God will be gracious to me, that my loved one may live.' "While there is life, there is hope; and while there is hope, there is room for prayer."[137] James reminds us that "the prayer of faith availeth much" (James 5:16).

I cannot bring him back. David was questioned with regard to a changed disposition once news arrived of the child's death. "His advisers were amazed. 'We don't understand you,' they told him. 'While the child was still living, you wept and refused to eat. But now that the child is dead, you have stopped your mourning and are eating again'" (2 Samuel 12:21 NLT). David exhibited hope until the end, praying, fasting and weeping, but ceased all when the child died. He realized, as every mother and father should, that praying, fasting and weeping could not bring the child back. Mourning in sorrow is healthy and beneficial. A helpful resource in the time of sorrow is my book *Grief Beyond Measure but Not Beyond Grace*.

I shall go to him. David's firm expectation of Heaven consoled him in the aftermath of the child's death. That expectation is never more clearly seen than in that grievous experience and the writing of Psalm 23, wherein he concludes, "I will dwell in the house of the LORD forever."

John MacArthur, referencing the death of David's son, said, "Here is the confidence that there is a future reunion after death, which includes infants who have died being reunited with saints who die."[138] C. H. Spurgeon said, "I rejoice to know that the souls of all infants, as soon as they die, speed their way to Paradise. Think what a multitude there is of them!"[139]

Matthew Henry comments, "Godly parents have great reason to hope concerning their children that die in infancy that it is well with their souls in the other world; for the promise is to us and to our seed, which shall be performed to those that do not put a bar in their own door, as infants do not."[140] He continues, "This may comfort us when our children are removed from us by death. They are better provided for, both in work and wealth, than they could have been in this world. We shall be with them shortly, to part no more."[141] A person becomes accountable for sin when ability develops to comprehend its presence, its power, its penalty, and the provision for its forgiveness (atonement and justification through the cross of Christ). The Christian parent can be confident of a grand reunion day with children who die before having attained this state or level of understanding.

41. How Much Knowledge Will Saints Possess in Heaven?

Newton said, "I do not know what I may appear to the world; but to myself I seem to have been only like a boy playing on the seashore and diverting myself in now and then finding a smoother pebble or a prettier shell than ordinary, while the great ocean of truth lay all undiscovered before me."[142] Like Newton, everyone, regardless of IQ, possesses a kindergarten level of knowledge in comparison to that which the saints have in Heaven. Knowledge presently is limited by our *finite* mind—the mental incapacity to know all things, understand all things and comprehend *all* that is knowable. Additionally, much of what is "known" is skewed and riddled with error and falsity due to faulty observation, interpretation and deception.

In Heaven our finite (limited) minds will become infinite (unlimited) minds, opening up full knowledge and understanding of all things. Paul writes, "Now we see things imperfectly, like puzzling reflections in a mirror, but then we will see everything with perfect clarity. All that I know now is partial and incomplete, but then I will know everything completely, just as God now knows me completely" (1 Corinthians 13:12 NLT). The *mirror* does not refer to modern mirrors made of glass for clear reflection but to the ancient kind made of polished metal which gave less clear reflection.[143] "To see a friend's face in a cheap mirror would be very different from looking at the friend" (Robertson and Plummer).[144] The contrast is clear between present understanding and knowledge (inferior mirror) and that which will be ours in Heaven (perfect mirror).

But then I shall know. "My knowledge shall be clear and distinct. I shall have a clear view of those objects which are now so indistinct and obscure. I shall be in the presence of those objects about which I now inquire; I shall 'see' them; I shall have a clear acquaintance with the divine perfections, plans, and character. This does not mean that he (we) would know 'everything,' or that he (we) would be omniscient."[145] No longer will there be the unexplained (the unexplainables of life will be understood), unknown, unclear (absence of confusion), unexpected and uncertain. This will negate the need to walk by faith in Heaven, as is the case on earth. See 2 Corinthians 5:7.

Faith will vanish into sight;
Hope will be emptied in delight;
Love in Heaven will shine more bright.

~ Christopher Wordsworth (1862)

The narrow grill or set of bars on the dungeon door admits only limited rays of light from the sky to the imprisoned. But let the dungeon door be opened and the prisoner set free, and he sees the whole of the heavens beaming with bright light, revealing ten thousand beauties unknown before. Just so will it be for the Christian who passes from this world (which now limits knowledge and insight) to Heaven.[146]

> No longer will there be the unexplained, unknown, unclear, unexpected and uncertain.

William Biederwolf said, "The brainiest men know a mighty little here, but up there our faculties will all be quickened and intensified, and all the pages of knowledge will unroll before us."[147] In Heaven God will touch our dull minds, enabling us to grapple with the infinite mysteries of the universe.[148] "All that hinders full excellence here will be absent there."[149] C. H. Spurgeon states, "The babe in Christ admitted to Heaven discovers more of Christ in a single hour than is known by all the divines of the assemblies of the church on earth."[150] The same preacher said, "I do not know that in Heaven they know *all* things—that must be for the Omniscient only—but they know all they need or really want to know; they are satisfied there."[151]

42. Why Don't Saints Go Immediately to Heaven When Saved?

It's because of the world's need to hear the Good News about Jesus' sinless life, sacrificial and vicarious death at Calvary, and triumphant resurrection three days later to make possible man's rightness with God. Were we transferred immediately to Heaven at salvation, the world would be void of the witnesses needed to bring the lost into the fold of God. While on earth, the Christian is to be Heaven's *light* to lighten earth's spiritual darkness, and *salt* to make it more palatable, and *witness* to point to Calvary.

43. What Will Be the Saint's Health in Heaven?

Look with me to Heaven through the lenses of Holy Scripture. There yonder standing fully erect at the Throne is Joni, who was a quadriplegic down here. Then see Fanny, who was blind, adoring Jesus and admiring Heaven's streets of gold, pearly gates and the foundation of its walls made of jasper, sapphire, emerald and other precious jewels. Up in Heaven's choir, there's Jim, who was dumb (unable to speak), singing loudly the praises of God for the first time. And behold Betty, the paralyzed child, now playing uninhibited on the streets of gold. Yet looking farther into the city, see David, who suffered greatly with cancer, now disease free and enjoying complete health. And, oh, what joy to see Ronald, who suffered with dementia, now "whole," communicating with family and friends. And yet the half has not been told of the restoration, yea, *newness* of health that its inhabitants experienced in the *twinkling of an eye* (1/300 of a second) at death.

I'll see all my friends in Hallelujah Square;
What a wonderful time we'll all have up there.
We'll sing and praise Jesus, His glory to share,
And you'll not see one [unwhole person] in Hallelujah Square.
~ Ray Overholt (1969)

No coronavirus, no migraines, no fevers, no high blood pressure, no high cholesterol, no body aches and pains, no uncontrollable body functions, no walking canes, no hospitals, no wheelchairs, and no practicing physicians, for they will be permanently retired. Isn't that stupendous!

Our bodies will be *glorified* in Heaven. Paul writes, "We're waiting the arrival of the Savior, the Master, Jesus Christ, who will transform our earthy bodies into glorious bodies like his own. He'll make us beautiful and whole with the same powerful skill by which he is putting everything as it should be, under and around him" (Philippians 3:21 MSG). See 2 Corinthians 5:2–5.

Joni Eareckson Tada observed from her wheelchair, "I haven't been cheated out of being a complete person—I'm just going through a 40-year delay, and God is with me even through that. Being glorified—I know the meaning of that now. It's the time, after my death here, when I'll be on my feet dancing."[152]

> On that resurrection morning
> When all the dead in Christ shall rise,
> I'll have a new body,
> Praise the Lord, I'll have a new life!
>
> Raised in the likeness of my Savior,
> Ready to live in Paradise,
> I'll have a new body,
> Praise the Lord, I'll have a new life.
> ~ Luther G. Presley (1887–1974)

44. Will Heaven Be a Blast or a Bore?

In *The Glory of Heaven,* John MacArthur states, "Many people think of Heaven as a bland, boring place with nothing enjoyable to do."[153] He explains: "The deep-seated suspicion that Heaven may be an eternal bore reflects the sinful thinking of fallen minds. As sinners we are naturally prone to think a little sin is surely more enjoyable than perfect righteousness. It is hard for us to imagine a realm wholly devoid of sin and yet filled with pure and endless pleasures. But that is exactly how Heaven will be."[154]

Paul Little agrees. "Heaven will not be the boring experience of strumming a harp on a cloud, as some facetiously characterize it. It will be the most dynamic, expanding, exhilarating experience conceivable. Our problem now is that, with our finite minds, we cannot imagine it."[155] Jon Courson makes a similar observation. "When Jesus says, 'I go to prepare a place for you,' He is not speaking generically, but specifically. Jesus is preparing a place for you specifically. Think through this. What do you enjoy? What has God built into your being? Whatever it is, know this. Jesus is preparing a place for you to fulfill the elements He's woven into the fabric of your personality uniquely and specifically."[156]

Don't endeavor to base Heaven's worship, service and fellowship on the present, for it will be exceedingly grander, far more exciting and enjoyable—it will reach thousands of times beyond our present experience or greatest imagination.

Lord Byron writes to the poet Moore, "I have been counting over the days when I was happy since I was a boy and cannot make them more than eleven. I wonder if I shall be able to make them a dozen before I die."[157] Happiness may be evasive now, but not in Heaven, for the psalmist gives assurance that 'in *His* presence is fullness of joy; in thy right hand there are pleasures forever' (Psalm 16:11).

45. Is It Possible for Saints to Be Too Heavenly-Minded to Be of Any Earthly Good?

The Bible instructs the believer to set his mind on the things above (where Christ sitteth, Heaven), not on things of the earth (Colossians 3:1–2). Can that be overdone? The short answer is a resounding no—because we have been given an earthly assignment with a Heavenly goal.[158]

The more the saint is consumed with Heaven's objective on earth (exalt Christ and populate Heaven) and its mandate (extend Divine invitations to go there), the greater *good* or value they become to earth. The one enables the other. Billy Graham wrote, "The more seriously we take Heaven, the more seriously we'll take our responsibilities on earth."[159]

46. Is It Possible for Saints to Be Too Earthly-Minded to Be of Any Heavenly Good?

Most sadly, the answer is true all too often due to lives lived in carnality. Carnality is the great sickness of evangelicals today. Paul addresses this serious soul condition in 1 Corinthians 3:1–4: "Brothers, I couldn't talk to you as spiritual people but as worldly people [*carnal*], as mere infants in the Messiah. I gave you milk to drink, not solid food, because you weren't ready for it. And you're still not ready! That's because you are still worldly. As long as there is jealousy and quarreling among you, you are worldly and living by human standards, aren't you? For when one person says, 'I follow Paul,' and another person says, 'I follow Apollos,' you're following your own human nature, aren't you? (ISV)."

> The carnal man, though saved, lives a life centered on the appetites of the flesh to the neglect of that which is spiritual.

The *carnal man*, though saved, lives a life centered on the appetites of the flesh to the neglect of that which is spiritual. Disobedient, thus dwarfed, this believer fails to grow, mature, or develop spiritually. He is a defeated Christian, not knowing the victory that walking under the control of the Holy Spirit enables, and is dependent upon another to do for him what he cannot or will not do spiritually—like a baby is dependent upon its parent.

Carnal Christians are "immature, without miracles, without wonders, lacking a wonderful sense of the presence of the Lord, held together by social activities and nothing else."[160] To be of value to Heaven, the Christian must be a *spiritual man*. See 1 Corinthians 2:15.

The spiritual man is the believer who lives under the control and dominion of the Holy Spirit. This believer continuously crucifies the lust of the flesh, the lust of the eyes, and the pride of life, denying self to the pleasure of the Lord. See Colossians 3:1–2; Luke 9:23.

47. Why So Little Talk and Excitement about Heaven?

Scripture teaches that saints ought to look forward to Heaven. Peter says, "But we are looking forward to the new Heavens and new earth he has promised, a world filled with God's righteousness" (2 Peter 3:13 NLT). But sadly, not many do look forward excitedly to Heaven. Adrian Rogers states, "If being a Christian and going to Heaven doesn't excite you, you have calluses on your soul."[161] Paul wrote, "Set your affection on things above, not on things on the earth" (Colossians 3:2). Baxter says, "There is nothing else that is worth setting our hearts on."[162]

> If being a Christian and going to Heaven doesn't excite you, you have calluses on your soul. ~ Adrian Rogers

Attachment to and preoccupation with the world (possessions, pleasures, people, popularity) suffocates intense longing for Heaven. Therefore, worldly stuff must be weaned out. The psalmist declared, "my soul is even as a weaned child" (Psalm 131:2). The Christian is to "wean" himself not only from worldly ambition but its sinful desires and pleasures. See 2 Corinthians 6:17.

The weaning is initiated at conversion, but because the Adamic nature yet remains, weaning continues throughout life. It takes inward struggle, battle and discipline to kill the old man and its lusts. As the baby fights to regain and retain the milk of the breast, the believer battles the return to (the pull of) fleshly "appetites." This is why even the godly Apostle Paul said, "I die daily" (1

Corinthians 15:31). Every day we must climb into the *electric chair of fleshly cravings* and die to their desire (wean ourselves from them).

C. H. Spurgeon observes, "When we think ourselves safely through the weaning, we sadly discover that the old appetites are rather wounded than slain, and we begin crying again for the breasts which we had given up. It is easy to begin shouting before we are out of the woods, and no doubt hundreds have sung Psalm 131 long before they have understood it."[163]

Unfamiliarity with Heaven breeds ignorant and often skewed views which lessen our desire for it. The more the believer sets his heart on Heaven through study, contemplation, and reflection on Heaven, the more excited and talkative he becomes about it.

In Baxter's classic *The Saint's Everlasting Rest,* he echoes my heart. His comments are lengthy but beg our attention. Baxter writes, "Why don't people seek this wonderful rest more enthusiastically? You would think that if a person heard even once about such a tremendous possibility, and if he believed what he heard, that he would almost forget to eat and drink and would care for nothing else but how to secure this treasure. And yet people who hear of it daily and profess to believe it as a fundamental article of their faith act as if they had never heard of any such thing or did not believe a word of it. They hardly talk about it, work for it, or think about it. And this is true not only of the worldly-minded, but even of devout Christians.

> And yet people who hear of it [Heaven] daily and profess to believe it as a fundamental article of their faith act as if they had never heard of any such thing or did not believe a word of it. They hardly talk about it, work for it, or think about it. ~ Richard Baxter

"Even the godly are too *lazy* when it comes to seeking their everlasting rest. We trifle away our time. *What a frozen stupidity has benumbed us!* We are dying, and we know it; yet we stir not. We do not make our eternal state the business of our lives. If I were not sick myself of the same disease, with what tears would I mix this ink in grieving over this universal deadness."[164]

O believer, have you forgotten the place of your true citizenship? If so, Paul informs you in Philippians of its locality: "But we are citizens of Heaven, where the Lord Jesus Christ lives. And we are eagerly waiting for him to return as our Savior. He will take our weak mortal bodies and change them into glorious bodies like his own, using the same power with which he will bring everything under his control" (Philippians 3:20–21 NLT). And it is there where our hearts should be fixed.

A stranger in the world below,
    I calmly sojourn here,
Nor can its happiness or woe
    Provoke my hope or fear.

Its evils in a moment end;
    Its joys as soon are past.
But, oh! the bliss to which I tend
    Eternally shall last.
~ Charles Wesley (1759)

Joseph Addison wrote, "In short, I would have everyone consider that he in this life is nothing more than a passenger and that he is not to set up his rest here but to keep an attentive eye upon that state of being to which he approaches every moment and which will be forever fixed and permanent."[165] Heartfelt (not just intellectual) understanding that you're just a pilgrim down here traveling to Heaven where Jesus awaits with all His glory ought to put you on shouting and testifying ground!

> 'Where I am, ye shall be also.' Let this inestimable privilege have its due effect upon us; let it stimulate our desires after Heaven.
> ~ Charles Simeon

Simeon summarizes, "How different was our Lord's address to unbelievers (John 8:21); but to believers he says, 'Where I am, ye shall be also.' Let this inestimable privilege have its due effect upon us; let it stimulate our desires after Heaven; let it reconcile us to the thoughts of death; let it engage us more earnestly to serve God (1 Thessalonians 1:9–10)."[166]

48. How Do Saints Cultivate Greater Longing and Joy for Heaven?

A greater thrill and joy for Heaven is derived in doing six things.

Be convinced of the reality and value of Heaven. You will never set your heart on Heaven or be excited about it until you count it the dearest and greatest treasure.

> The baptized life means that the Christian is seeking Heaven and is thinking Heaven. His feet are upon the earth, but his head is with the stars. He is living like a citizen of Heaven here on earth. ~ A.T. Robinson

Talk about Heaven more and more. Let Heaven be the theme of conversations and the songs of the heart. The more saints speak or sing about Heaven, the less likely they will *forget it* and/or fail to be profited by the *hope* it promises. Paul admonishes saints: "Set your mind and keep focused habitually on the things above [the Heavenly things], not on things that are on the earth [which have only temporal value]" (Colossians 3:2 AMP). A. T. Robertson writes: "The baptized life means that the Christian is seeking Heaven and is thinking Heaven. His feet are upon the earth, but his head is with the stars. He is living like a citizen of Heaven here on earth."[167]

Allow earthly happenings to prompt remembrance of Heaven. As I write, a pandemic (for which there is no known cure) is sweeping the world (coronavirus), sickening millions and killing thousands. In such times, it's good to remember that our homeland in Heaven is free from such diseases that cause sickness, suffering and death. In hearing good news, be prompted to praise God for the good news that Jesus is soon coming to take the saints home to Heaven. Let the joy of fellowship with friends be a reminder of the perfect, unbroken fellowship that awaits in Heaven. Upon growing fatigue in labor for the Master, remember that a sabbath day of rest awaits in Heaven. May church worship services ignite excitement in knowing that in Heaven such adoration will be ceaseless. Keep associating happenings with Heaven so that your contemplation of that glorious abode not only brings strength and comfort but increases excitement in going there.

Read books, listen to music and sermons that focus on Heaven. Flood the mind with its beauty and blessing and benefits. Meditate upon Scripture that depicts Heaven. See Isaiah 25:8–12; John 14:1–6; Revelation 7:13–17; Revelation 21:4–8; Revelation 22:3–9.

To repeat C. S. Lewis' observations in *Mere Christianity,* "If you read history you will find that the Christians who did the most for the present world were just those who thought most of the next. It is since Christians have largely ceased to think of the other world that they have become so ineffective in this."[168]

Contemplate its closeness. Heaven is not far away, even for the youngest. But its closeness is more easily grasped by the oldest. Knowing that it is not very far away—a year, month, week, day, hour—let us be stirred to think and muse over it more.[169]

I am a pilgrim here within a foreign land;
My home is far away upon a golden strand.
Ambassador for Thee of realms beyond the sea,
I'm here on business for my King.

~ Elijah T. Cassel (1902)

Don't be shy or cowardly about Heaven. C. S. Lewis stated, "We are very shy nowadays of even mentioning Heaven. We are afraid of the jeer about 'pie in the sky' and of being told that we are trying to 'escape from the duty of making a happy world here and now into dreams of a happy world elsewhere.' But either there is 'pie in the sky' or there is not. If there is not, then Christianity is false, for this doctrine is woven into its whole fabric. If there is, then this truth, like any other, must be faced, whether it is useful at political meetings or not."[170] Since Heaven is a reality, as Jesus taught, the saint ought to *speak about it often, regardless of sneers or surroundings or audience.*

49. How Can Sinners Hope to Get to Heaven?

Heaven is the eternal dwelling place of the redeemed family of God. The *entrance ticket* into this celestial city is not church membership, baptism, confirmation, righteousness, or good deeds, but a personal relationship with Jesus Christ through the new birth (John 3:3; Acts 20:21). George Swinnock said, "Heaven must be in you before you can be in Heaven."[171]

Jesus, in discussing His ascension to Heaven to make preparation for the saints, was asked by Thomas to clarify the way to the celestial abode (John 14:5). Jesus answered him, "I am the way, the truth, and the life: no man cometh unto the Father, but by me" (John 14:6). In essence, Jesus is saying that He is the only *Door* to this celestial city (John 10:9), for He is not simply "the way," but is *the* Way to eternal life in the Father's House.

Understanding this truth, the disciples referred to their following of Jesus as *the* Way (Acts 19:9, 23). Further, Jesus validates His claim as being "the Way" by asserting that He is the embodiment of all Truth (Ephesians 4:21) and is the giver of abundant, fulfilling and eternal life (1 John 5:12; John 10:9).

Heaven is the believer's Home. To go to this Home, you must be part of His family. And the only way to be part of His family is to be born into it.[172] Do you recall the story of Nicodemus? Jesus forthrightly said to him, "Marvel not that I said unto thee, Ye must be born again" (John 3:7). See John 1:12. The New Testament church consists of the family of God.

> I'm in this church, this glorious church.
> I didn't join; no I was born. I've had a new birth.
> Some glorious day, I will sail away.
> It's by grace, not by works; I'm in this church. ~ Joel Hemphill

Jesus' desire is for everyone to be with Him in Heaven. He paid the great price at Calvary to make it possible. But it remains up to man whether he goes to Heaven or not. He must choose to receive Christ Jesus as Lord and Savior. Jesus said, "I tell you, Nay: but, except ye repent, ye shall all likewise perish" (Luke 13:5).

> Only one answer will give a person the certain privilege, the joy, of entering Heaven. "Because I have believed in Jesus Christ and accepted him as my Savior." ~ Billy Graham

Billy Graham said, "Only one answer will give a person the certain privilege, the joy, of entering Heaven. 'Because I have believed in Jesus Christ and accepted him as my Savior.'"[173]

Here in this world, He bids us come;
There in the next, He shall bid us welcome. ~ John Donne

50. What Calms the Saint in the Hour of Death?

"Precious in the sight of the LORD is the death of his saints" (Psalms 116:15). He calls the death of a saint precious—"His saints," those engraved upon the palms of His hands, endeared to His heart and fully justified by Calvary's blood. Certainly, this strange description of death is not easy for us to grasp when it has snatched our loved one. But understanding why it's counted precious helps. It is *precious* to the Lord, for it means that another one of the souls which He redeemed is safe at Home, delivered from evil and the evil one.

Death is a certain and an uncertain step. Certain in that all will take it. Uncertain as to when it will be taken and how. See 1 Samuel 20:3. No man except Elijah and Enoch had or has a "bridge" over death's "dark sullen stream" to Heaven—not even Jesus.

In dying, the saint's faith is tested to its utmost, for it is to take a step into that which is known theologically but unknown experientially. To know as Job did, that man, upon death, will live again, is the "game changer" in confronting it (Job 14:14). If faith is weak regarding dying, then Jude says 'build it up' (Jude 20). How is that done? The Bible makes plain that faith is *built up* through the intake of the Word of God. Paul says, "Consequently, faith comes from hearing the message, and the message is heard through the word about Christ" (Romans 10:17 NIV). Being a faithful student of the Scriptures is the surest means of increasing one's faith.

Matthew Henry states, "The believing hopes of the soul's redemption from the grave and reception to Glory are the *great support and joy of the children of God in a dying hour*. They hope that God will redeem their souls from the power of the grave, which includes the preserving of the soul from going to the grave with the body. The grave has a power over the body by virtue of the sentence (Genesis 3:19), and it is cruel enough in executing that power (Song of Solomon 8:6); but is has no such power over the soul. It has power to silence and imprison and consume the body, but the soul then moves and acts and converses more freely than ever (Revelation 6:9, 10); it is immaterial and immortal."[174] Charles Simeon states, "Through His atoning blood you may look forward to death and judgment with far other eyes than they can be viewed by the ungodly world. You may regard death as the commencement of life and the very gate of Heaven."[175]

But even with strong faith, the process of dying can be frightful. Knowing that, God provides a *new grace for dying*. The Bible says, "So let us come boldly to the throne of our gracious God. There we will receive his mercy, and *we will find grace to help us when we need it most*" (Hebrews 4:16 NLT). Dying grace is that which grants comforting assurances from the Lord, enabling the Christian to boldly and fearlessly make the transfer from this life into the next. *It is dispensed when one is dying, not when he is in health*. Living grace is provided for life (Acts 4:33), dying grace for death (2 Corinthians 12:9). Rest assured, beloved saint, that in the hour in which *dying grace* is needed, it shall be abundantly provided.

There's been grace for every trial;
There's been grace for every mile;
   There's been grace sufficient from his vast supply—
Grace to make my heart more tender,
Grace to love and pray for sinners,
   But there'll be new grace when it's my time to die.

Grace not yet discovered,
Grace not yet uncovered,
   Grace from his bountiful store,
Grace to cross the river,
Grace to face forever—
   There'll be new grace I've not needed before. ~ Tom Hayes

C. H. Spurgeon said, "Even death itself, with all its terrible influences, has no power to suspend the music of a Christian's heart, but rather makes that music become more sweet, more clear, more Heavenly, till the last kind act which death can do is to let the earthly strain melt into the Heavenly chorus, the temporal joy into the eternal bliss!"[176] John R. Rice shares words of comfort to the dying: "We will not step out into the dark when we leave this world. But as the lost sheep feels so secure on the shepherd's shoulders, so all God's children are clasped safely in the hand of Christ and no one can take us away from Him. He wants us to be with Him."[177]

How glorious and wonderful that Jesus describes Heaven in a *homey* way: "My Father's house." Death often terrorizes. The unknown of what lies beyond the grave only intensifies that terror and fear, causing dread and despair. After all, nobody comes back. Even great saints that have assurance of salvation often draw back at death. We have the knee-jerk reaction of horror when the subject of death is raised. "But the words 'my Father's house' gives us a gleam in the gloom."[178]

Walking home from work at night was a terror to a boy. That which prompted the fear was the cemetery through which he had to pass to reach home on its other side. In fact, the light of home was visible. Suddenly the boy thought, *Why should I be afraid of walking through the cemetery when I see the light of home and I know my father is watching for me to arrive safely.* Death and the cemetery hold no fear for the saint, for he sees the Light shining brightly from the *Father's house* on the other side and knows the Father awaits to receive him *home* safely.

Come and go with me to my Father's house,
To my Father's house, to my Father's house.
Come and go with me to my Father's house;
There is joy, joy, joy!

Peace and happiness in my Father's house,
In my Father's house, in my Father's house—
Peace and happiness in my Father's house,
There is joy, joy, joy! ~ Unknown

"Beloved, it is very probable that we shall have such a sight of our glorious King as we never had before when *we come to die.* Many saints in dying have looked up from amidst the stormy waters and have seen Jesus walking on the waves of the sea and heard Him say, 'It is I, be not afraid.' Ah, yes! when the tenement begins to shake and the clay falls away, we see Christ through the rifts, and between the rafters the sunlight of Heaven comes streaming in. But if we want to see face to face the "King in his beauty," we must go to Heaven for the sight, or the King must come here in person. Oh, that He would come on the wings of the wind!"[179]

My peace I give when there's but death at the door for thee—
The gateway is the cross to get to me.[180]
~ Streams in the Desert

51. If Not Heaven, Where Do People Go at Death?

In Revelation 20:15 we are told that anyone whose name was not recorded in the Lamb's Book of Life "was cast into the lake of fire." God says, "The wicked shall be turned into hell" "where their worm dieth not, and the fire is not quenched" (Psalm 9:17; Mark 9:44). Clearly the Bible teaches there is a Hell to shun just as much as there is a Heaven to gain at life's end. You can't have the one without the other (universalism believes there is only a Heaven), for both are teachings rooted deeply in the infallible Word of God.

Hell was designed for Satan and the fallen angels, not man (Matthew 25:41). "But God is so gracious," states Paige Patterson, "that He never coerces anyone to make Him the object of his affection and adore Him. If there is rejection of His overtures, then the only option is the place called Hell."[181] Charles Stanley says, "Unbelievers go to Hell because they are incompatible with Heaven. They don't go to Hell to pay God back. The severity of their sin doesn't send them there. The quantity of their sin doesn't send them there. The problem is that they aren't suited for Heaven. They have not been cleansed of the sin that makes them unholy."[182] And nothing impure or unholy may enter that Holy City. The Bible says, "But nothing unclean will ever enter it, nor anyone who does what is detestable or false, but only those who are written in the Lamb's book of life" (Revelation 21:27 ESV). The only way to become "clean and holy," fit to enter Heaven, is through the soul-purifying blood of the Lord Jesus Christ. Hear the Word of God and believe: "Then he told me, 'These are those who have come through the great oppression: *they have washed their robes and made them white in the blood of the Lamb.* That is why they now have their place before the throne of God, and serve him day and night in his temple. He who sits upon the throne will be their shelter. They will never again know hunger or thirst. The sun shall never beat upon them, neither shall there be any scorching heat, for the Lamb who is in the center of the throne will be their shepherd and will lead them to springs of living water. And God will wipe away every tear from their eyes'"

(Revelation 7:14 PHILLIPS). See Ephesians 1:7; Revelation 1:5; Hebrews 9:22 and Hebrews 10:19.

To go to Hell, the sinner must climb over every roadblock erected by a loving God on his path—Calvary's love, sermons, churches, soul winners, ministers, the Word of God, the persistent prayers of a loving mother and others, and a convicting conscience. On the path to Hell, the blood of Jesus is trampled upon by the sinner every step of the way, and it ceaselessly and compassionately cries out, "My love for you was demonstrated at the cross. I died and rose again so that you wouldn't go to Hell but would join me in Heaven instead." See Romans 5:8; John 3:16.

52. Is Jesus the Only Person of the Trinity We'll See in Heaven?

The answer is yes. W. A. Criswell says, "There is one God, and only one. We shall not see three gods in heaven. The only God there is, is God."[183] Jesus said unto him, "Have I been so long a time with you, and yet hast thou not known Me, Philip? He that hath seen Me hath seen the Father; and how sayest thou then, 'Show us the Father'?" (John 14:9). In John 10:30 Jesus said, "I and my Father are one." See Revelation 5:12.

53. What Is the Christian's Hope in Death?

The Christian has hope (confidence) that at life's end a better world awaits. The saint shuts his eyes in death and opens them instantly in Heaven (2 Corinthians 5:8). "The wicked is driven away in his wickedness: but the righteous hath hope in his death" (Proverbs 14:32).

At death, the believers' hope is for *gain*. Paul said, "For to me to live is Christ, and to die is gain" (Philippians 1:21). The Christian's hope (confident trust; assurance) is to gain freedom from sin, sorrow and suffering; fellowship supreme with Jesus and Heaven's citizens;

incomparable joy and peace; reunion with loved ones; and rest from service and spiritual warfare. Jonathan Edwards comments, "To go to Heaven, fully to enjoy God, is infinitely better than the most pleasant accommodations here."[184] Matthew Henry states, "The righteous then have the grace of hope in them; though they have pain, and some dread of death, yet they have hope. They have before them the good hoped for, even the blessed hope which God, who cannot lie, has promised."[185] In contrast, the wicked will meet death in his sin (its guilt, shame, judgment) and be cast into outer darkness for it ("The wicked is driven away in his wickedness"). His estate at death only moves from bad to worse, whereas for the saint his estate changes from good to far better.

John R. Rice said, "Those who go to Heaven ride on a pass and enter into blessings that they never earned, but all who go to Hell pay their own way."[186] John Knox remarks, "When the wicked is paid in his own coin, there is an end of him; at death's door, the just still hope."[187]

54. Can the Saint Be Sure That Christ Has the Power to Keep His Promises about Heaven?

Yes, most certainly! Christ conquered the grave, proving Himself to be Victor over death and sin and Hell. The angel said to the two women on Easter morning at the empty tomb, "He is not here: for he is risen, as he said. Come, see the place where the Lord lay" (Matthew 28:6).

The empty tomb is *a place of Investigation*. 'Come and see; His body is not here.' It was not stolen but raised from the dead. Despite the efforts of the chief priests, Pharisees and Pilate to keep His body in the tomb by having it guarded by Roman soldiers (trained fighting men of the highest order); covering the mouth of it with a gigantic stone (far too heavy for a few men to roll away, and if they could it would create such a loud noise as to alert the soldiers) and affixing the Roman seal to it (anyone tampering with the seal would be executed). But, despite the best effort of these enemies of Christ, on Easter morning the stone was supernaturally rolled away, and up from the grave He arose, the Victor over the dark domain.

It is a *place of Documentation*. It documents Jesus' fulfillment of the many prophecies concerning the Messiah made hundreds of years earlier. God told us *before* it happened (through prophecies) so we might believe it *after* it happened. The resurrection of Christ is a fact established by the clearest and most verifiable evidence. The vacant tomb documents that what He said of Himself did indeed happen. Prior to His death at Calvary, Jesus said, "Destroy this temple, and in three days I will raise it up" (John 2:19). And on Easter morning it happened *just as He said*. More than a dozen appearances to many hundreds of people give added verification to His resurrection.

It is *a place of Edification*. Come and see and learn what the resurrection of Christ means. It affirms Jesus' deity, that He indeed is the Son of God who has power over death and authority to keep every promise ever made to His followers. It affirms His power to raise our dead bodies from the grave. The Bible says, "But in fact, Christ has been raised from the dead. He is the first of a great harvest of all who have died" (1 Corinthians 15:20 NLT). Jesus made a thoroughfare out of what was a dead-end street. And because He lives, we shall live also (John 14:19). It means salvation's plan was complete and accepted by the Father in Heaven. It assures the saints will meet up with loved ones who died in the Lord. And what a great reunion day that will be! The Bible says, "We believe that Jesus died and that He rose again. So, because of Him, God will raise with Jesus those who have died" (1 Thessalonians 4:14 NCV).

It is *a place of Exhortation*. The angel instructs the women, and all who "see what they saw" through the lens of faith and historical and biblical documentation, to 'go quickly and tell his followers that Jesus has risen from the dead' (Matthew 28:7). And they did, and we must. *They ran* to share the good news. And so must we, for it's the news of hope that a hurting world sorely needs to hear and heed.

It is *a place of Celebration.* We are told that the ladies departed from the empty tomb of Jesus "with…great joy" (Matthew 28:8). The Easter message fills the heart with great joy. Fear is replaced with peace that overflows in joy. The Christian, because of the empty tomb, now bravely and confidently can look "death" in the eye, saying, "O death, where is thy sting? O grave, where is thy victory" (1 Corinthians 15:55). Through His resurrection Christ removed the stinger of fear, anxiety, dread and hopelessness out of death for the redeemed. If that doesn't turn a pouting Christian into a shouting Christian, then there is something wrong with his "shouter."

> Through His resurrection Christ removed the stinger of fear, anxiety, dread and hopelessness out of death for the redeemed.

It is *a place of Invitation.* As the angel invited the women to come and see, so Jesus invites you. Come and see and believe and receive Him by faith as Lord and Savior and live abundantly and live eternally. Jesus invites, "Come unto me, all ye that labor and are heavy laden, and I will give you rest. Take my yoke upon you, and learn of me; for I am meek and lowly in heart: and ye shall find rest unto your souls" (Matthew 11:28–29). See Revelation 22:17.

The hope of Easter and the Christian church is that life continues beyond the grave in Heaven. But it's more than a hope, now that Christ has risen from the dead; it is a certainty.

His resurrection is man's game changer in this life and the life which is to come. It is our surety that all His promises about Heaven will be kept. "I am he that liveth, and was dead; and, behold, I am alive for evermore, Amen; and have the keys of hell and of death" (Revelation 1:18). His empty tomb is our pledge and assurance that our grave will also one day be empty.

55. Will There Be Marriage in Heaven?

The answer is found straight from the mouth of Jesus in Mark 12:25: "For when they shall rise from the dead, they neither marry, nor are given in marriage; but are as the angels which are in heaven." Forthrightly Jesus says in Heaven marriage is unnecessary, therefore nonexistent. He doesn't give an explanation except to say that in Heaven we will be "as the angels" who do not marry or procreate. Note, Jesus is not saying we will be as the angels in identity (become angels), but that we will be like them in nature—eternal beings that do not marry. Only in that regard do saints resemble angels in Heaven.

They neither marry, nor are given in marriage. J. D. Grassmick says, "Marriage is necessary and suitable for the present world order, in which death prevails, in order to continue the human race. But angels, whose existence the Sadducees denied (Acts 23:8), are deathless and live in a different order of existence where they have no need for marital relations or reproduction of offspring. Their lives center totally around fellowship with God. So it will be in the afterlife for human beings rightly related to God."[188] Herschel Hobbs writes, "People often ask me if they will know their loved ones in Heaven. My reply is that they knew them on earth and that stripped of the limitations of the flesh they will have more intelligence in Heaven than they had on earth. This does not mean my wife will be my wife in Heaven (Matthew 22:30). As children of God we will have a relationship far richer and sweeter than any we knew on earth."[189]

To summarize, Jesus' words do not mean that those who were married on earth will not recognize each other as their spouses in Heaven, for they will. It's the marriage relationship that ceases, not the memory of it. J. Vernon McGee writes, "This doesn't mean that a man and a woman who were together down here can't be together in Heaven."[190]

56. Are Saints Going to Eat and Drink in Heaven?

The resurrected Christ ate fish and honey (Luke 24:37–43). The eschatological banquet of the redeemed is depicted as an eating and drinking affair at the Lord's table (Luke 22:30). Jesus says that in Heaven He will give the saints the right to eat of the tree of life (Revelation 2:7) that bears twelve different kinds of fruits and produces fruit every month (Revelation 22:2). Jesus told the disciples that He would not drink the fruit of the vine again until He drank it (new fruit of the vine) in the Kingdom of God (Mark 14:25). Jesus also said that people (the redeemed) will come from the four corners of the earth to *feast* at the Lord's table in Heaven (Luke 13:29).

Based upon the limited information Scriptures reveal about food and drink in Heaven, I believe saints will be eating fruits from its twelve-fruit-bearing evergreen tree and drinking new fruit of the vine. What else may be on the menu is unknown but certainly will be the best dishes and drinks imaginable, for it's the King's table, and He is the host. It will be a *feast* to behold and enjoy!

The reason that the resurrected Christ ate food with the disciples was not to satisfy hunger (such is nonexistent in the glorified state) but for proof of His resurrection and fellowship. Likewise, eating and drinking in Heaven will be for fellowship with the King and the saints.

57. What Is Jesus Doing in Heaven?

Christ Jesus is not merely seated in Heaven enjoying its blessedness. So what is He doing?

Christ is ruling. Presently from Heaven's throne He reigns (rules), thwarting evil, saving sinners, vindicating His name, answering prayers and protecting saints. His power is incomparable and unconquerable. See Psalm 93:1. He is ever observing and controlling the affairs of the world and watching over His children.

Christ is interceding. He is seated at the right hand of God the Father, ever interceding in our behalf (Hebrews 1:3). See Hebrews 4:14–16; Hebrews 7:25; Romans 8:34. An intercessor is one who pleads or entreats in behalf of another. What does that mean? Jesus defends us against Satan's accusations before God about our sin (like he made against Job in Job 1:6–12). The accusations are of no avail, because Jesus procured our forgiveness of sin by paying the debt of sin owed in full at Calvary. When Jesus died for man, He *imputed* (transferred) man's sin upon Himself and *imputed* (transferred) His perfect righteousness to man. This "Great Exchange" enables God to see us without fault, blameless and thus acceptable. See 1 Peter 2:24 and 2 Corinthians 5:21.

> Jesus paid it all; all to him I owe.
> Sin had left a crimson stain;
> He washed it white as snow.
>
> ~ Elvina Mable Reynolds Hall (1822–1889)

But Christ's intercession for the saints is specific also (focused upon the exact need at the time—to provide 'help in the hour of need,' like comfort, peace, guidance, deliverance, forgiveness, vindication, etc.) and preventative (purpose-driven prayer to keep us from falling into sin, becoming the prey of the evil one, making bad decisions, and to enable us to persevere). See 1 John 2:1.

"It is a consoling thought," states Louis Berkhof, "that Christ is praying for us, even when we are negligent in our prayer life; that He is presenting to the Father those spiritual needs which were not present to our minds and which we often neglect to include in our prayers; and that He prays for our protection against the dangers of which we are not even conscious, and against the enemies which threaten us, though we do not notice it. He is praying that our faith may not cease, and that we may come out victoriously in the end."[191]

Robert Murray McCheyne said, "If I could hear Christ praying for me in the next room, I would not fear a million enemies. Yet the distance makes no difference; He is praying for me."[192]

> If I could hear Christ praying for me in the next room, I would not fear a million enemies. Yet the distance makes no difference; He is praying for me. ~ Robert Murray McCheyne

Albert Barnes summarizes Christ's Heavenly role in the believer's behalf: "He does in Heaven whatever is necessary to obtain for us grace and strength; secures the aid which we need against our foes; and is the pledge or security for us that the law shall be honored, and the justice and truth of God maintained, though we are saved."[193]

The endless intercession, pleading, praying, defending Jesus does in our behalf is ever successful. He is a "lawyer" (advocate) that never loses a case.

Christ also is preparing Heaven. "I go to prepare a place for you" (John 14:2). Through His death, resurrection and ascension, Jesus has prepared a place in Glory for the redeemed. All of Heaven's host is being prepared for the saint's arrival.

Christ is preparing for His coming. "I will come again, and receive you unto myself; that where I am, there ye may be also" (John 14:3). The next event on Heaven's calendar is His return to earth to take the saints to their glorious Home. See 1 Thessalonians 4:16–17; Revelation 1:7.

58. Will Deathbed Confessions of Faith Avail for Heaven?

Are deathbed conversions possible? Can a person live his entire life in sin and rejection of Jesus Christ and be saved in life's final moments? What sayeth the Word of God?

Scripture clearly teaches that whoever, whenever may be saved (Romans 10:13). John Calvin remarks, "There is...no room to doubt that [Christ] is prepared to admit into His kingdom all, without exception, who shall apply to him."[194] Doubt about the validity of deathbed conversions is generated by thoughts that good works have something to do with genuine salvation, which they clearly do not, based on the Bible (Titus 3:5–6; Ephesians 2:8–9; Romans 3:24).

Luke records the first deathbed conversion of the Bible, and it was genuine. To the penitent thief on the Cross, Jesus said, "Today shalt thou be with me in paradise [Heaven]" (Luke 23:43). It clearly reveals that the most wicked may be saved at the brink of death. It's better to come late to Heaven's gate than not to come at all.

Having said that, it is expedient to make clear that a person ought not to gamble on having an opportunity for such a conversion. Many deaths are sudden, unexpected, providing no chance of salvation in the last hour. Additionally, there is danger that if such a deathbed confession does occur, it may be based entirely on fear, not on genuine repentance. To ensure that neither is the case, a person should here and now receive Christ (John 1:12).

It is my joy to have experienced "deathbed" confessions. Whether genuine or not I do not know, for evidence of such (transformation, change; see 2 Corinthians 5:17) was not forthcoming due to immediate death. I accepted them as real based upon what sincerity of heart and repentant attitude was manifested. Scripture encourages saints to seek the lost up to and in their final moments of life, even as Christ did with the penitent thief, in an effort to save them from the jaws of Hell.

59. Do Saints in Heaven Pray?

Reference to saints praying in Heaven is found in Revelation 6:10: "And they cried with a loud voice, saying, How long, O Lord, holy and true, dost thou not judge and avenge our blood on them that dwell on the earth?" Clearly the martyrs in Heaven prayed (talking to God is synonymous with praying to God) for God to execute justice on earth with regard to their murderers. God heard and answered the prayer (Revelation 8:3–4). See Revelation 5:13; 7:9–10.

60. Who Are the Angels in Heaven?

Numerous poems, songs and teachings about angels are skewed with error, for they are based on the writer's or singer's imagination or perspective. All that is known about angels is revealed in Scripture. There have been no special revelations about angels outside God's Word.

Angels are created, spiritual beings who are God's "messengers," and they are mentioned some 280 times in the Bible, mostly in the New Testament. Wuest says, "The angels were created before this universe was brought into existence through the creative act of God, for they shouted for joy at the beauty of the original creation (Job. 38:7)."[195] "Where were you when I laid the foundations of the earth? Tell me, if you know so much. Do you know how its dimensions were determined, and who did the surveying? What supports its foundations, and who laid its cornerstone as the morning stars sang together and *all the angels shouted for joy*?" (Job 38:4–7 TLB).

There are three types of angels: cherubim (Genesis 3:24), seraphim (Isaiah 6:2), and hosts ("the LORD God of hosts"). At times they become visible in human form (Hebrews 13:2). Angels are holy (Revelation 14:10); created (Genesis 1:1; Nehemiah 9:6; Colossians 1:16); eternal (Luke 20:36); incessantly working (Revelation 4:8); great in knowledge (2 Samuel 14:17); swift and mobile (Daniel 9:20–23); happy and joyous (Luke 15:10); great in power and strength but are not omnipotent (2 Kings 19:35; 2 Samuel 24:16); God's helpers in judging; worshippers (Revelation 4:8); servants to the body of Christ on earth—helpers, defenders, protectors, encouragers (Genesis 19:15; Psalm 78:49; 91:11; Luke 4:10); celibate, not given in marriage (Matthew 22:30); in complete submission to God (1 Peter 3:22; Psalm 103:20); numerous (Revelation 5:11; Daniel 7:10; Psalm 68:17; Hebrews 12:22); announcers of Christ's second coming (Matthew 24:31; 1 Thessalonians 4:16); comforters (Daniel 10:19; Acts 27:24; Matthew 1:20; 28:5–6; Judges 6:12; 1 Kings 19:5); verbal communicators (1 Corinthians 13:1; Acts 1:10–11); assigned to individual believers (Matthew 18:10); called by "personal" names (Luke 1:19; Jude 9); strengtheners of believers (Luke 22:43; Exodus 23:20); different in rank (Michael possesses the most authority); deliverers (Numbers 20:16); instructors (Acts 8:26; 10:3–5); resistors of the Devil (Jude 9) and are the saints' companions forever (Revelation 5:9–13).[196]

> Angels remind us of the unseen world, where Satan and his demonic host work, battling the kingdom of God (Ephesians 6:12), and God works, thwarting those efforts through sundry means invisible to man (2 Kings 6:16–20).

Angels remind us of the *unseen world*, where Satan and his demonic host work, battling the kingdom of God (Ephesians 6:12), and God works, thwarting those efforts through sundry means invisible to man (2 Kings 6:16–20). Research and study for this writing has "opened" my eyes wider to the unseen spiritual world; may it do the same for the reader.

C. H. Spurgeon comments about angels, "Loyalty to their Lord leads them to take a deep interest in the children of His love; they rejoice over the return of the prodigal to his father's house below, and they welcome the advent (arrival) of the believer to the King's palace above."[197] Bear in mind that *absolutely* everything angels say or do is authorized and commanded by God. They never work on their personal initiative, only at God's bidding. Their ultimate purpose is to magnify and glorify God continuously, not bring attention to themselves.

61. Do the Angels in Heaven Pray for the Saints on Earth?

Billy Graham said that the Bible doesn't say the angels pray for us. That could be because "One far greater than the angels already is praying for us: the Lord Jesus Christ. He alone is the divine Son of God, who even now sits in Heaven interceding for us (Hebrews 7:25)."[198]

Angels are dispatched by God in answering prayer occasionally. See Daniel 9:21–23. Daniel made request and God graciously sent answer by the angel Gabriel. A similar experience occurs in Daniel 10:11–14. The angel Gabriel delivers word to Zechariah from God in answer to his prayer. "Then an angel of the Lord appeared to Zechariah, standing on the right side of the incense table. When he saw the angel, Zechariah was startled and frightened. But the angel said to him, 'Zechariah, don't be afraid. God has heard your prayer. Your wife, Elizabeth, will give birth to a son, and you will name him John'" (Luke 1:11–13 NCV).

The bottom line is that Scripture is mute about angels praying for saints. And what it is silent about, man can only speculate about. What is known is that they are eagerly ready to assist God in answering our prayers.

62. What Kind of Service Do Angels Perform for Saints on Earth?

Angels are "ministering spirits" to the redeemed (Hebrews 1:14). The Greek word for *minister* refers to "serviceable labor and assistance."[199] "They are ministering spirits, or Heavenly assistants, who are continually active today in building the body of Christ— advancing the ministry of Jesus and the building of His church."[200] Their earthly assignment is to benefit the redeemed church of God. McDonald says, "They [angels] serve those who are saved from the penalty and power of sin but not yet saved from the presence of sin; that is, those believers who are still on earth."[201]

They are God's messengers to do as He bids. The psalmist says, "Bless the LORD, ye his angels, that excel in strength, that do his commandments, hearkening unto the voice of his word" (Psalm 103:20). God sent the angel Gabriel to assist Daniel (Daniel 9:21), Zacharias (Luke 1:19) and Mary (Luke 1:26). Note, angels are not servants *of* the church, but Christ's servants *to* the church.[202] "Praise the Lord, all you warriors [angels] of his, you servants [angels] of his who carry out his desires" (Psalm 103:21 NET).

Biblical references to angels ministering to saints include Lot (Genesis 19), Elijah (1 Kings 19:4–8), Elisha (2 Kings 6:16, 17), Daniel (Daniel 6:22; 9:20–27; 10:10–21), Zacharias (Luke 1:11–20), Mary (Luke 1:26–38), the shepherds (Luke 2:9–14), Mary Magdalene and other women (Luke 24:4–7; John 20:11–13), the apostles immediately after the ascension (Acts 1:10, 11), the apostles in prison (Acts 5:19, 20), Peter (Acts 12:7–10), Paul (Acts 27:23, 24). Angels ministered to Christ in the wilderness of temptation (Matthew 4:11) and in Gethsemane (Luke 22:43).[203]

Angels perform various services in behalf of the Lord to the saint (see an overview in Question 60, "Who Are the Angels in Heaven?"). Here I mention several specifically.

They escort saints from earth to Heaven at death. Lazarus at his death "was carried by the angels into Abraham's bosom [Heaven]" (Luke 16:22). David Jeremiah says, "For every Christian, the time is coming when we will move into our Heavenly homes, assisted by the Lord's real estate agents—called angels. After carefully studying this subject in the Bible, I believe that angels take believers home to Heaven when we die and help us move into our new houses. This is tremendously comforting, and it takes much of the intimidation out of the move."[204]

They protect saints. Hebrews 1:14 TLB says, "No, for the angels are only spirit-messengers sent out to help and care for those who are to receive his salvation." Their great power and strength ("excel in strength") safeguard the saint against the wiles of the Devil, adversaries and mishaps. The psalmist declared, "For he will order his angels to protect you wherever you go" (Psalm 91:11 NLT). C. H. Spurgeon states, "If our eyes could be opened, we should see horses of fire and chariots of fire about the servants of the Lord; for we have come to an innumerable company of angels, who are all watchers and protectors of the seed-royal."[205] See Psalm 34:7 and Psalm 91:11–12. Angels are dispatched by God especially in times of emergency to warn, help and/or protect the saints (Daniel 6:22). "Much of their work is to oppose the malice of evil spirits, who seek our hurt, and to defend us from their rage and subtlety (deceptiveness; skill to be unnoticeable)."[206] See Revelation 12:7, 9; Matthew 4:11; 1 Thessalonians 2:18.

Billy Graham states, "Angels guide, comfort, and provide for people in the midst of suffering and persecution."[207] "When struggling against overwhelming difficulties," states F. B. Meyer, "when walking the dark, wild mountain pass alone; when in peril or urgent need, we are surrounded by invisible forms like those which accompanied the path of Jesus, ministering to Him in the desert, strengthening Him in the garden, hovering around His cross, watching His grave, and accompanying Him to His Home. They keep pace with the swiftest trains in which we travel. They come unsoiled through the murkiest air. They smooth away the heaviest difficulties. They garrison with light the darkest sepulchers. They bear us up in their hands, lest we should strike our foot against a stone. Many an escape from imminent peril, many an unexpected assistance, many a bright and holy thought whispered in the ear, we know not whence or how, is due to those bright and loving spirits."[208]

> Many an escape from imminent peril, many an unexpected assistance, many a bright and holy thought whispered in the ear, we know not whence or how, is due to those bright and loving spirits. ~ F. B. Myer

They observe saints. Paul says, "Instead, I sometimes think God has put us apostles on display, like prisoners of war at the end of a victor's parade, condemned to die. We have become a spectacle to the entire world—to people and angels alike" (1 Corinthians 4:9 NLT). It is uncertain if glorified saints can see saints on earth, but angels certainly do and serve as their encouragers and helpers. Perhaps the glorified saints know of earthly affairs from the angels.

They comfort saints. An angel comforted and strengthened Daniel. Daniel 10:19 NLT records the encounter: "'Don't be afraid,' he said, 'for you are very precious to God. Peace! Be encouraged! Be strong!' As he spoke these words to me, I suddenly felt stronger and said to him, 'Please speak to me, my lord, for you have strengthened me.'" See Acts 27:24 and Matthew 1:20; 28:5–6.

A mother's only child accidentally fell into a fire and was so severely burned that he died only hours later. A minister rushed to the mother's side once the word was received of the child's accident and death. Surprisingly, he found the mother calm. The mother shared with him how she had wept bitterly by her son's bed, when suddenly he exclaimed, "Mother, don't you see the beautiful man who is standing there and waiting for me?" Time and again the child persisted in saying that "the beautiful man" was waiting for him. The mother testified her son seemed ready and even anxious to go to him. The mother's heart was strangely comforted and cheered by the presence of the guardian angel.[209]

They show saints how to worship. Angels constantly worship God night and day in exemplary fashion. "And let all the angels of God worship Him" (Hebrews 1:6). "And all the angels were standing around the throne and around the elders and the four living creatures; and they fell on their faces before the throne and worshiped God, saying, 'Amen, blessing and glory and wisdom and thanksgiving and honor and power and might, be to our God forever and ever. Amen.'" (Revelation 7:11–12 NAS). Saints, though ministered unto by angels, have no authority over them; only God does. It is God that gives angels instructions, not man. Scripture says, "For he will command his angels to protect you in all your ways" (Psalm 91:11 ISV).

63. Do Saints Have Guardian Angels?

Two Scripture texts indicate the *saint* (not unbeliever) in fact has a guardian angel that watches over him. In Matthew 18:10, Jesus states that children have "their angels" that are on standby to care for them at the Lord's command. The second text is Acts 12, where an angel freed Peter from prison. Afterward, Peter knocked on the door of a house where a prayer meeting for his release was ongoing. In discovering it was Peter, the servant, due to being overcome with excitement, unthinkingly left him outside while she ran to tell the others the good news. The praying saints, however, counted the person at the door as Peter's angel. Strangely, though they were praying for Peter's release, they didn't believe it when it happened! How like them are saints today—prayers are uttered without faith that what is asked will be done.

Billy Graham shares in the book *Angels, God's Secret Agents* an interesting story. "The Reverend John G. Paton, a missionary in the New Hebrides Islands, tells a thrilling story involving the protective care of angels. Hostile natives surrounded his mission headquarters one night, intent on burning the Paton's out and killing them. John Paton and his wife prayed all during that terror-filled night that God would deliver them. When daylight came, they were amazed to see the attackers unaccountably leave. They thanked God for delivering them. A year later, the chief of the tribe was converted to Jesus Christ, and Mr. Paton, remembering what had happened, asked the chief what had kept him and his men from burning down the house and killing them. The chief replied in surprise, 'Who were all those men you had with you there?' The missionary answered, 'There were no men there, just my wife and I.' The chief argued that they had seen many men standing guard—hundreds of big men in shining garments with drawn swords in their hands. They seemed to circle the mission station so that the natives were afraid to attack. Only then did Mr. Paton realize that God had sent His angels to protect them. The chief agreed that there was no other explanation. Could it be that God had sent a legion of angels to protect His servants whose lives were being endangered?"[210] See a similar incident recorded in 1 Kings 6:14–17. Graham testifies that at moments of special need, he was attended to by angels.[211]

George Washington said that his success at Valley Forge was due to "an inspiring visit from a Heavenly being" (guardian angel). Experience with angels is indisputable when what is experienced is based not on the concoctions of man but on the Word of God. Christians ought not to fear when opposing evil, knowing there are multitudes of angels appointed to assist.

64. Should Angels Be Worshipped?

"Angels do, indeed, have a ministry," writes Jon Courson, "but the ministry is to us. They're not to be exalted or worshiped by us."[212] Heavenly angels worship God incessantly and refuse worship offered to them. Upon receiving the glorious vision of Heaven on the Isle of Patmos, John fell at the feet of the angel. The angel reprimanded him, saying, "See that you do not do that! I am your fellow servant, and of your brethren who have the testimony of Jesus. Worship God! For the testimony of Jesus is the spirit of prophecy" (Revelation 19:10 NKJV). See Colossians 2:1–23.

65. Are Demons Really Fallen Angels?

The angels (one-third of the angelic host—Revelation 12:4) that joined Satan in the rebellion in Heaven were cast out (evicted) with him (Revelation 12:9; Isaiah 14; Ezekiel 28). These fallen angels now are demons. The names *fallen angels* and *demons* are synonymous and are used interchangeably in the Bible (Revelation 12:7–9).[213]

Fallen angels are also called devils, evil and unclean spirits. Satan accuses (slanders) man before God, as in the case of Job, and he and the host of demons attack (deceive and tempt) man on earth. Though roaming the whole earth seeking whom they may devour, as a roaring lion hungry for prey (1 Peter 5:8), Satan and demons are limited in their work. These evil adversaries cannot touch a Christian without God's permission. Satan could not afflict Job (Job 2:6) or Peter (Luke 22:31) without God's permission.

Although Satan was thrown out of Heaven, his communication with God continued (Job 2:6; Luke 22:31). The Bible says that Hell ("eternal fire"—Jude 7) was "prepared for the devil and his angels" (Matthew 25:41). "The devil is delighted to be denied!" states Jack Taylor. "He doesn't want to be given credit for a job well done! He resists detection."[214]

How will Satan and the demons be vanquished? It is in and through the "blood of the Lamb" (Revelation 12:11). "There is power, power, wonder-working power in the blood of the Lamb." It has redeeming power (Ephesians 1:7), cleansing power (1 John 1:7), preserving power (Revelation 7:15; Romans 8:1), entering power (Hebrews 4:16; Ephesians 2:13), peace-giving power (Colossians 1:20), and overcoming power (Revelation 12:11).

> By the blood of Christ the Victor
> Overcome the enemy;
> By its virtue and its power
> You will win the victory.

> By the blood of Christ the Victor
> Counter him who doth accuse;
> By the blood for you defending
> All the sland'rer's blame refuse.

By the blood of Christ the Victor
    God's sure faithfulness believe;
Through the blood of your Redeemer
    God's forgiveness now receive.

By the blood of Christ the Victor
    Your position now declare;
Through the blood, prevailing ever,
    All His vict'ry fully share.

By the blood of Christ the Victor
    Claim His full authority;
Just apply the blood of Jesus
    And defeat the enemy.

By the blood of Christ the Victor
    Standing in the Heavenlies,
In the pow'r of Christ ascended,
    Tread the principalities.

       ~ Lowell Mason (1792–1872)

Oswald Sanders says, "The prayer warrior must learn how to plead the victory of Calvary, for the blood of the Lamb has forever broken the power of the Devil and robbed him of his prey. Plead the blood of the Lamb for the liberation of the soul for whom you pray."[215] "Seeing then that our victory over this great adversary is to be gained by the blood of the Lamb, let us exercise faith in that blood."[216]

Ultimately, Satan and the demons will be vanquished, permanently banned from earth. The war that began in Heaven by Satan and the rebellious angels and that continues on earth will climax at Armageddon with Christ with His angelic army victorious.[217] See 2 Peter 2:4.

66. Is It Possible for Saints in Heaven to Sin?

John Bunyan said, "Oh! what acclamations of joy will there be when all the children of God shall meet together without fear of being disturbed by the antichristian and Cainish brood!"[218]

The biblical description of Heaven includes the absence of sin. John writes, "But nothing unclean will ever enter it, nor anyone who does what is detestable or false, but only those who are written in the Lamb's book of life" (Revelation 21:27 ESV). See Isaiah 52:1. The Bible says, "There will no longer exist anything that is cursed [because sin and illness and death are gone]" (Revelation 22:3 AMP). *No longer exist anything that is cursed!* G. K. Beale says, "The curse of physical and spiritual death set on the human race by Adam in the first garden is permanently removed by the Lamb."[219] That Heavenly land will be free of every evil that the curse of sin placed on man: separation from God, opposition, persecution, intimidation, adversities and death.

> The saint will sin and pray repentantly for the last time while on earth.

Heaven is the throne room of God and glistens with perfection. Man's adamic nature (sinful) is completely destroyed upon entering Heaven, giving place to the dominion of the new nature (righteousness, holiness, purity) in Christ Jesus. Thus, Heaven is void of any trace of sin or temptation or inclination to sin. The saint will sin and pray repentantly for the last time while on earth. God will not judge sin anymore, since it does not exist in His holy house.[220] "No wish, no desire, no hunger towards that which is unclean shall ever be found in the perfect city of God. Nor even a thought of evil can be conceived there, much less a sinful act performed."[221]

Heaven is a holy place
Filled with glory and with grace—
Sin can never enter there;
All within its gates are pure,
From defilement kept secure—
Sin can never enter there.

If you hope to dwell at last,
When your life on earth is past,
In that Home so bright and fair,
You must here be cleansed from sin,
Have the life of Christ within—
Sin can never enter there.

You may live in sin below,
Heaven's grace refuse to know,
But you cannot enter there;
It will stop you at the door,
Bar you out forevermore—
Sin can never enter there. ~ Charles W. Naylor (1899)

In hearing of a land which is free from the cause and curse of sin, we sympathize with John in his saying, "Even so, come, Lord Jesus" (Revelation 22:20).

67. Is It Biblical to Pray to Saints in Heaven?

Unequivocally the Bible teaches that prayer is to be addressed *only* to God. In Matthew 6:9 the disciples are instructed to pray, "Our Father which art in Heaven." Paul instructed the church in Rome to offer their "prayers to God" (Romans 15:30). David testified to God, "Unto thee will I pray" (Psalm 5:2). Moses joins David in ascertaining that he 'prayed to the Lord' (Numbers 21:7). Paul himself made his 'prayer unto God' (Romans 10:1; Ephesians 3:14).

"And another angel came and stood at the altar with a golden censer, and he was given much incense to offer with *the prayers of all the saints* on the golden altar before the throne, and the smoke of the incense, with the prayers of the saints, rose before God from the hand of the angel" (Revelation 8:3–4 ESV). Wiersbe comments, "The 'prayers of the saints' are not prayers given through the saints in Glory. In Revelation 5:3, no man was found worthy to open the book save Jesus Christ; so why should we pray through any other name? These prayers are the prayers of God's people: 'Thy kingdom come!'"[222]

> There is no instance or mention in Scripture where saints are told to pray to or worship someone other than God.

There is no instance or mention in Scripture where saints are told to pray to or worship someone other than God. In fact, it reveals that when man sought to worship genuine saints, it was rejected. In Acts 10:26, Peter instructed Cornelius, who bowed at his feet, to get up. Peter said, "Stand up! I am only a man like you" (ERV). When a crippled man was healed, the crowd began to worship Paul and Barnabas. They responded, "Friends, why are you doing this? We are merely human beings—just like you! We have come to bring you the Good News that you should turn from these worthless things and turn to the living God, who made Heaven and earth, the sea, and everything in them" (Acts 14:15 NLT). In Revelation 19:10, the angels refused the worship of man.

Christians have direct access to the throne of God. The writer of Hebrews says, "Let us go with complete trust to the throne of God. We will receive His loving-kindness and have His loving-favor to help us whenever we need it" (4:16 NLV). Further, Hebrews declares that Jesus Christ intercedes for the saints: "Wherefore he is able also to save them to the uttermost that come unto God by him, seeing he ever liveth to make intercession for them" (7:25). See Question 57, "What Is Jesus Doing in Heaven?"

With Jesus Christ as Mediator (1 Timothy 2:5) and Intercessor (Hebrews 7:25) for saints, there is no need for another. And for that reason, there isn't any other.

68. Will the Saint Be Judged in Heaven?

There are two separate and different judgments that will occur at the coming of Christ. The *Great White Throne Judgment* (Revelation 20:11–15) is for the unbeliever (all whose names are not recorded in the Book of Life), whereas the *Judgment Seat of Christ* (2 Corinthians 5:10; Romans 14:12; 1 Corinthians 3:11–15) is strictly for the redeemed.

The unbeliever will be judged according to his sinfulness and rejection of Christ. This will result in his eternal separation from God in the Lake of Fire. It will show Christ to be fair and just (Acts 17:31).

The believer's judgment (takes place in Heaven) is not to deem the believer worthy or unworthy to enter Heaven (he will be there). It has nothing to do with salvation and entrance into Heaven. That already will have been established on earth through the new birth (John 3:15–16). *Tickets* to Heaven were purchased at a great cost by Jesus but provided without charge to all who receive Him as Lord and Savior. See Romans 8:1; Titus 3:5; Ephesians 2:8–9.

Then for what is the saint to be judged? All believers, without exception, will give an accounting for their works (Romans 14:12; 2 Corinthians 5:10). No believer will be permitted to give *answer* for another or plead *excuses* for another. Masks will fall off, and the fakery and deception displayed in life will be known. We all shall be seen for *what* we are in heart (meaning of "appear" in 2 Corinthians 5:10). That which shall be examined includes not only our actions, but also our words, thoughts, inclinations, motives and dispositions.[223] "Every act of man leaves its mark, and hereafter our life will be judged by these marks."[224] The judgment will take into consideration the believer's abilities, gifts, talents, capabilities, and opportunities. Its overarching purpose is to reward faithfulness and devotion through the presentation of five crowns, and assign positions or Heavenly assignments to the saints.

At our court date in Heaven it will be far too late to wish that we had taken the Christian life and commitment to Christ more seriously. The time to do that is now. So walk, work and witness that you may receive a "full reward" on that day (2 John 8).

69. Are Believers Their Brothers' Keepers in Regard to Heaven?

The short answer is yes. Christians are compelled by Christ to share the good news of Heaven with people regardless of their race, face or place. All are invited to the Father's House, but all must have a "ticket" to enter. And the Bible states that although the ticket was a costly purchase for Christ (tormenting crucifixion), it's offered free to all who will accept it. Our task is to make the *ticket* available.

In *The Weight of Glory,* C. S. Lewis says, "There are no ordinary people. You have never talked to a mere mortal. Nations, cultures, arts, civilizations—these are mortal, and their life is to ours as the life of a gnat. But it is *immortals whom we joke with, work with, marry, snub, and exploit*—immortal horrors or everlasting splendors." Believers are to exhaust every means to bring others to Christ that they too may escape Hell's "immortal horrors" and gain Heaven's "everlasting splendors."[225]

Saints are God's watchmen to warn man of impending judgment and damnation. Ezekiel says, "Human, I now make you a watchman for Israel. Any time you hear a word from My mouth, warn them for Me. When I say to the wicked, 'You will surely die,' you must warn them so they may live. If you don't speak out to warn the wicked to stop their evil ways, they will die in their sin.

But I will hold you responsible for their death" (Ezekiel 3:17–18 NCV).

Old Testament major cities posted a watchman atop a tall tower on the wall to maximize his view of the surrounding territory.[226] Upon an enemy's approach, he was to blow the trumpet loudly to warn the city. However, if he was negligent in his duty and the enemy brought havoc to the city's inhabitants, the blood of those that died would be on his hands.

> Failure to warn family, friends, neighbors, classmates, workmates, etc., of impending doom in the lake of fire (Hell) is gross negligence for which God will hold us personally responsible.

Using this symbolism, God says to Christians, "I have appointed you a watchman to the world." The lesson is plain. We are our brothers' keepers and responsible for telling them about Jesus Christ. Failure to warn family, friends, neighbors, classmates, workmates, etc., of impending doom in the lake of fire (Hell) is gross negligence for which God will hold us personally responsible. Don't let others die without warning. Don't let them die untold. Don't die with their blood on your hands.

70. Is It Wrong to Be Homesick for Heaven?

It's not wrong; in fact, it is completely natural for soldiers on foreign soil defending our nation's freedom to be homesick for home and family because that's their greatest treasure. They think and talk much about home, sorely miss families and friends at home, expectantly and excitedly anticipate going home and greatly rejoice in the news that they will soon be going home. They are homesick for home.

If this is normal for a soldier, it's most certainly spiritually and mentally right and natural for the child of God to feel this way with regard to his Heavenly Home. After all, our citizenship is not of this present world but in that beautiful Land beyond the sky, even sweet Beulah land. "But we are citizens of Heaven, where the Lord Jesus Christ lives" (Philippians 3:20 NLT).

Jesus taught, "For where your treasure is, there your heart [your wishes, your desires; that on which your life centers] will be also" (Matthew 6:21 AMP). Heaven is where our heart is, for there is where our treasure is (family, friends, peace, joy, health, sinlessness, perfection). But the dearest treasure of Heaven to the saint is Jesus. "Mere acquaintance with correct doctrine," wrote A. W. Tozer, "is a poor substitute for Christ, and familiarity with New Testament eschatology will never take the place of a love-inflamed desire to look on His face."[227]

Paul was homesick for Heaven. He writes, "And we are *eagerly waiting* for him to return as our Savior. He will take our weak mortal bodies and change them into glorious bodies like his own, using the same power with which he will bring everything under his control" (Philippians 3:20–21 NLT). Underscoring this longing for Home, again he says, "I am torn in two directions—on the one hand I long to leave this world and live with Christ, and that is obviously the best thing for me. Yet, on the other hand, it is probably more necessary for you that I should stay here on earth" (Philippians 1:23–24 PHILLIPS).

But Christians at large don't embrace Paul's passion for Heaven. John MacArthur states, "Because the church doesn't really have Heaven on its mind, Christians tend to be self-indulgent, self-centered, weak, and materialistic. Our present comforts consume too much of our thoughts, and if we've not careful, we end up entertaining wrong fantasies about Heaven—or thinking very little of Heaven at all."[228]

C. H. Spurgeon, in the sermon *The Voice of Heaven,* said, "Jesus beckons thee to the skies, believer. Lay not fast hold upon the things of earth. He who is but a lodger in an inn must not live as though he were at home. Keep thy tent ready for striking. Be thou ever prepared to draw up thine anchor and to sail across the sea and find the better port, for while Jesus beckons, here we have no continuing city."[229]

> Jesus beckons thee to the skies, believer. Lay not fast hold upon the things of earth. He who is but a lodger in an inn must not live as though he were at home. Keep thy tent ready for striking. Be thou ever prepared to draw up thine anchor and to sail across the sea and find the better port, for while Jesus beckons, here we have no continuing city. ~ C. H. Spurgeon

In answer to the question, "Is it wrong to be homesick for Heaven?" Billy Graham said, "No, it isn't wrong. In fact, if we never yearn for Heaven, it may mean we've become too satisfied or too preoccupied with our lives right now!"[230]

I'm kind of homesick for a country
To which I've never been before.
No sad good-byes will there be spoken,
For time won't matter anymore.

Beulah Land, I'm longing for you,
And someday on thee I'll stand.
There my Home shall be eternal—
Beulah Land, sweet Beulah Land.

I'm looking now across the river
Where my faith will end in sight.
There's just a few more days to labor,
Then I will take my Heavenly flight. ~ Squire Parsons

So in unison with Paul, may all the family of God on earth say, "So we do not look at what we can see right now, the troubles all around us, but we look forward to the joys in Heaven which we have not yet seen. The troubles will soon be over, but the joys to come will last forever" (2 Corinthians 4:18 TLB).

71. What Ought Saints to Do until Heaven?

Live thoughtfully. Keep your mind on Heaven. See Colossians 3:1–2. Never cease to think of its glories and benefits that await the saint in that Heavenly Land.

Live expectantly. Never allow the "music" of Heaven to be drowned out by the pressures, pursuits, pains and pleasures of life. Live with anticipation of soon being in that Heavenly domain.

Live calmly. Until we reach Home, there is much that might stir panic, fear and terror in man's heart. But with their hearts fixed on Jesus and Heaven, saints will experience serenity and calmness regardless of the trial. They don't fret, fear, or become downcast. God declares to all His children, "'For the mountains may depart and the hills be removed, but my steadfast love shall not depart from you, and my covenant of peace shall not be removed,' says the LORD, who has compassion on you" (Isaiah 54:10 ESV). God gives us peace in the midst of life's storms, a peace the world simply cannot understand. And perhaps He allows them, our trials and troubles, to keep us homesick for Home. See Philippians 4:7.

Live holily. Solomon compares the believer's progression in sanctification to the advancing of the sun (Proverbs 4:18). The Christian is saved in an instant (sunrise), but godliness is progressive (as the sun rises in the sky) until clothed with Christ's perfection in Heaven (sun reaches noonday).

A grave contradiction exists when one states the fact of personal salvation and yet is content to continue in the old life of sin (2 Corinthians 5:17). Alexander Maclaren says, "The intention [of] every Christian life should be a life of increasing luster, uninterrupted, and the natural result of increasing communion with and conformity [continuous growth] to the very fountain itself of Heavenly radiance."[231]

Live tellingly. Tell what awaits the saint in Heaven. Tell how to prepare for entering there. And once you tell it, tell it again and

99

again. Offer a "free ticket" to Heaven to all that will accept it through faith and repentance.

Christ arose and to Heaven went—
Tell the Good News; tell the Good News.
All may follow who repent—
Tell the Good News; tell the Good News. ~ Gene Bartlett

Live joyfully. Jesus said, "Notwithstanding in this rejoice not, that the spirits are subject unto you; but rather rejoice, because your names are written in heaven" (Luke 10:20). Happiness is based upon what happens *to* you. Joy is based upon what happens *in* you. Despite the worst the world may throw at us, we are able to rejoice. Why? Our names are recorded in the Book of Life. That reality puts fuel in the saints' joy tank. See Philippians 4:4.

Live devotedly. Walk in submission to the Lord in service, sacrifice, stewardship, and separation. Love Him supremely and honor Him continuously in walk, thought and talk. See Romans 12:1–2.

72. Why Didn't Jesus Tell Us More about Heaven?

C. H. Spurgeon offers an answer to the question, stating, "It is very little that we can know of the future state, but we may be quite sure that we know as much as is good for us. If God wills for us not to know, we ought to be satisfied not to know. Depend on it; He has told us all about Heaven that is necessary to bring us there, and if He had revealed more, it would have served rather for the gratification of our curiosity than for the increase of our grace."[232]

God chose to leave many things about Heaven unrevealed. There are some things that we could not comprehend, others that are simply unspeakable. ~ Adrian Rogers

100

Spurgeon's explanation is supported by Adrian Rogers, who said, "God, in all his wisdom, chose to leave many things about Heaven unrevealed. There are some things that we could not comprehend, others that are simply unspeakable (2 Corinthians 12:4). What we do know, however, is that Heaven is a place where we will need nothing more, want nothing more than to worship Jesus for eternity."[233] "Eye hath not seen, nor ear heard, neither have entered the heart of man, the things which God hath prepared for them that love him. But God hath revealed them unto us by his Spirit" (1 Corinthians 2:9–10). Matthew Henry states, "There are things which God hath prepared for those that love Him and wait for Him. There are such things prepared in a future life for them, things which sense cannot discover, no present information can convey to our ears, nor can yet enter our hearts."[234]

My knowledge of that life is small,
The eye of faith is dim,
But 'tis enough that Christ knows all
And I shall be with Him. [235]

Alexander McLaren hammers the question's answer home: "But we know as much as we need. We know that God is there. We know that it is the Father's House. We know that Christ is in it. We know that the dwellers there are a family. We know that sweet security and ample provision are there; and for the rest, if we needed to have heard more, He would have told us."[236]

73. What Will Our Departure to Heaven Be Like?

T. De Witt Talmage, in the sermon "The Ferryboat of the Jordan" (2 Samuel 19:18), likens the believer's departure from earth to Heaven to the transportation of David and his family from one side of the river Jordan to the other. Aptly he states that the ferryboat had to be sent from the other side by the tribe of Judah.

Praise God, there is a ferryboat named mercy, grace and salvation that God is sending from the other side for the redeemed. Man-made Heavenbound vessels on this side (morality, self-righteousness, ordinances, religious piety) will shipwreck in the journey. Note that the King along with his household was aboard the ferry. The presence of the king aboard assured the passengers that the utmost precautions had been taken to insure safe travel.

Talmage continues, "When a soul goes to Heaven, it does not go alone. The King is on board the boat. Was Paul alone in the last exigency [the finale of life]? Hear the shout of the scarred missionary as he cries out, 'I am now ready to be offered up, and the time of my departure is at hand.' Was John Wesley alone in the last exigency? No. Hear him say, 'Best of all, God is with us.' Here is the promise: 'When thou passeth through the waters, I will be with thee, and through the rivers, they shall not overflow thee.' Christ at the sick pillow to take the soul out of the body, Christ to help the soul down the bank into the boat, Christ midstream, Christ on the other side to help the soul up the beach—be comforted about your departed friends. Be comforted about your own demise when the time shall come. Tell it to all the people under the sun that no Christian ever dies alone. The King is in the boat."[237]

> Be comforted about your departed friends. Be comforted about your own demise when the time shall come. Tell it to all the people under the sun that no Christian ever dies alone. The King is in the boat. ~ T. De Witt Talmage

Knowing not only that the King has sent a *ferry* for our exodus into the next world but that He is aboard should calm our fears, end our trembling and marshal confident assurance that the trip will be successful. The saint with this knowledge can shout to death, "O death, where is your victory? O death, where is your sting? For sin is the sting that results in death, and the law gives sin its power. But thank God! He gives us victory over sin and death through our Lord Jesus Christ." (1 Corinthians 15:55–57 NLT).

74. Does God Speak to Man from Heaven?

Never have I heard His audible voice, but I have with all certainty heard Him speak in five primary ways in my life. The Bible says that the prerequisite for hearing God's "voice" is knowing Him through a personal relationship with His Son, the Lord Jesus Christ (John 18:37). Jesus said, "My sheep hear my voice, and I know them, and they follow me" (John 10:27).

He speaks through *Holy Scriptures*. The inspired Word of God, the Bible, is God's voice to man (2 Timothy 3:16). As it is read, He Himself is saying to us that which we are reading. Christ speaks to man through the testimonies of His eyewitnesses, through His life and through the pages of Scripture (Hebrews 1:1–2). "Thy word is a lamp." Consider its distance (it is a divine light and shines from Heaven to earth and earth to Heaven), its duration (it has been shining for over 4,000 years and will continue until the return of Christ), and its direction (it points or guides from darkness [sin] into the light [righteousness]).

He speaks through *Holy Men*. Holy ministers are they who walk in closeness to God and relay His messages from the Scriptures to the saints. Faithful clergymen are God's mouthpieces on earth.

He speaks through *Holy Companions*. Intimate friends may communicate God's plan or directive for our life in times of uncertainty. In past days long-distance phone calls could be placed person to person or station to station. God sometimes "phones" us station to station, that this, through a second party.

He speaks through a *Holy Conscience*. Often God will speak to us by His Holy Spirit through the conscience concerning an activity or attitude, prodding us to restraint and giving us direction. A seared or defiled conscience often blocks our hearing when He prods (1 Timothy 4:2). Thus a holy and sensitive conscience is imperative if we are to hear the Holy Spirit. "And the only thing that keeps our conscience sensitive to Him," writes Oswald Chambers, "is the habit of being open to God on the inside."[238]

He also speaks through *Holy Creation*. Nature is not defiled by sin the way man is and therefore remains "holy." David declared, "The heavens proclaim the glory of God. The skies display His craftsmanship. *Day after day they continue to speak;* night after night they make Him known" (Psalm 19:1–2 NLT). See Romans 1:20. Nature reveals God's existence and glory through its magnificent wonder and beauty. Its intrinsic design, complexity and order speak to man about its Creator and Master Designer.

To hear God speak, the ears must be tuned to His frequency and trained to hear His voice.

75. Who Has Ascended and Descended from Heaven?

The question is asked by Agur in Proverbs 30:4. The most educated and brightest unbeliever is incapable of answering the question herein posed, "for they are foolishness unto him: neither can he know them, because they are spiritually discerned" (1 Corinthians 2:14). The question was answered by Jesus in John 3:13: "And no man hath ascended up to heaven, but he that came down from heaven, even the Son of man which is in heaven." In Ephesians 4:9–10, Paul reveals that *Jesus likewise descended:* "Now that he ascended, what is it but that he also descended first into the lower parts of the earth? He that descended is the same also that ascended up far above all heavens, that he might fill all things." Here we discover the Gospel proclaimed in the Old Testament.

What enormous, pregnant truth is found in Jesus' descent from and ascension to Heaven! In Jesus' own words, the reason for His descent to earth was "to seek and to save that which was lost" (Luke 19:10). Man's salvation and reconciliation to God necessitated Jesus' agonizing and tormenting death upon the cross. Peter explains, "For Christ also hath once suffered for sins, the just for the unjust, that he might bring us to God, being put to death in the flesh, but quickened [made alive again] by the Spirit" (1 Peter 3:18).

Three days after His crucifixion and burial, He was raised from the dead, which was verified by many witnesses. Forty days later, *Jesus ascended* back into Heaven. "And when he had spoken these things, while they beheld, he was taken up; and a cloud received him out of their sight. And while they looked stedfastly toward heaven as he went up, behold, two men stood by them in white apparel; Which also said, Ye men of Galilee, why stand ye gazing up into heaven? this same Jesus, which is taken up from you into heaven, shall so come in like manner as ye have seen him go into heaven" (Acts 1:9–11).

> Christ came down to earth to be the Mediator between man and God (1 Timothy 2:5). Upon completion of the work (procurement of salvation for man through the cross), He ascended back into Heaven.

H. A. Ironside summarizes Jesus' ascension: "Jesus, His work finished and His ministry on earth accomplished, ascended of His own volition, passing through the upper air as easily as He had walked upon the water. The fact of His having gone up and having been received by the Shekinah—the cloud of divine Majesty— testifies to the perfection of His work in putting away forever the believer's sins. When Jesus was on the tree, Jehovah 'laid on Him the iniquity of us all' (Isaiah 53:6). He could not be now in the presence of God if one sin remained upon Him. 'Wherefore he saith, When he ascended up on high, he led captivity captive, and gave gifts unto men' (Ephesians 4:8). He had destroyed 'him that had the power of death, that is, the devil' (Hebrews 2:14)."[239] Jesus' deity is proclaimed in Proverbs 30:4. He came down to earth to be the Mediator between man and God (1 Timothy 2:5). Upon completion of the work (procurement of salvation for man through the cross), He ascended back into Heaven (Acts 1:11). The church awaits His glorious return (John 14:2–3).

76. What Are Man's Two Possible Eternal Destinies?

There are but two paths on which a person may choose to walk. The Bible says, "But the path of the just is as the shining light, that shineth more and more unto the perfect day. The way of the wicked is as darkness: they know not at what they stumble" (Proverbs 4:18–19).

One path is that which leads to the city of Zion (Heaven, v. 18); the other leads to eternal banishment from the presence of God (Hell, v. 19). The one is lit with the brilliancy of Christ; the other is enveloped in darkness. The saved in Heaven will be in a domain where there is no darkness, for God is the Light of the City (Revelation 21:23); the lost will be in Hell where there is nothing but the blackness of darkness forever (Jude 13). The same truth is uttered by Jesus in Matthew 7:13–14: "Enter ye in at the strait gate: for wide is the gate, and broad is the way, that leadeth to destruction, and many there be which go in thereat: Because strait is the gate, and narrow is the way, which leadeth unto life, and few there be that find it."

C. H. Spurgeon says, "What I am when death is held before me, that I must be forever. When my spirit goes, if God finds me hymning His praise, I shall hymn it in Heaven; doth He find me breathing out oaths, I shall follow up those oaths in Hell. Where death leaves me, judgment finds me. As I die, so shall I live eternally."[240]

77. Who Shuts the Door to Heaven?

Jesus Christ has absolute control over admittance of anyone to Heaven. Since it is His Kingdom Home, He has the authority to prescribe the conditions; He can include and exclude man based on those terms.[241] See Revelation 3:7. This makes it explicitly clear that no priest, minister or church has the authority to "grant" admission into Heaven or to keep one out.

A time has been set in the future by the Lord when the door to Heaven will be eternally shut, allowing no more admission. The door on Noah's ark, prior to the fierce judgment of God upon the world, was not closed by Noah. It was *shut* by God (Genesis 7:16). The word "shut" means to "close" in an absolute sense. People left outside the ark suffered the wrath of God in judgment (death). Their grievous pleadings, screaming and knocking to be permitted entrance was of no avail. It is a picture of the end of time (Matthew 24:37–39). See 1 Peter 3:20–21. Once Christ shuts the door to Heaven, it's too late for man's prayers and penitence. That's why Paul exhorts, "For God says, 'Your cry came to me at a favorable time, when the doors of welcome were wide open. I helped you on a day when salvation was being offered.' Right now God is ready to welcome you. Today he is ready to save you" (2 Corinthians 6:2 TLB).

78. What Have Saints Said at Death's Door?

May the last words and/or glimpses of Heaven or angels that great saints witnessed in life's final moments comfort, cheer, encourage and assist every child of God in removing the fear of death. Review of what was said and seen is in no wise contradictory of Scripture teaching.[242]

"Let me die the death of the righteous, and
let my last end be like his!"
Numbers 23:10

C. H. Spurgeon. "Can this be death? Why, it is better than living!"

William Wilberforce. "My affections are so much in Heaven that I can leave you all without regret; yet I do not love you less, but God more."

Brownlow North. "'The blood of Jesus Christ his Son cleanseth us from all sin'—that is the verse on which I am now dying. One wants no more."

Isaac Watts. "It is a great mercy that I have no manner of fear or dread of death. I could, if God please, lay my head back and die without terror this afternoon."

George Whitfield. "Lord Jesus, I am weary *in* Thy work, but not *of* Thy work. If I have not yet finished my course, let me go and speak for Thee once more in the fields, seal the truth, and come home to die."

George Washington. "Doctor, I am dying...but I am not afraid to die."

Lady Powerscourt. "One needs a great many Scriptures to live by, but the only Scripture that a person needs to die by is 1 John 1:7; and that verse never was sweeter to me than at this moment."

Benjamin Abbot. "Glory to God! I see Heaven sweetly opened before me!"

Martha McCrackin. "How bright the room! How full of angels!"

Phillip Heck. "How beautiful! The opening Heavens around me shine!"

John Owen. "When John Owen, the great Puritan, lay on his deathbed, his secretary wrote [in his name] to a friend, 'I am still in the land of the living.' 'Stop,' said Owen. 'Change that and say, I am yet in the land of the dying, but I hope soon to be in the land of the living.'"

John A. Lyth. "Tell them I die happy in Jesus!"

Augustine. "Your will be done. Come, Lord Jesus!"

John Pawson. "I know I am dying, but my deathbed is a bed of roses. I have no thorns planted upon my dying pillow; Heaven is already begun!"

Stonewall Jackson. "Let us cross the river and rest in the shade."

R. G. Lee. "I see Heaven! Oh...I didn't do it justice! I see JESUS! I didn't do HIM justice!"

Billy Graham (in his final column). "By the time you read this, I will be in Heaven, and as I write this I'm looking forward with great anticipation to the day when I will be in God's presence forever. I'm convinced that Heaven is far more glorious than anything we can possibly imagine right now, and I look forward not only to its wonder and peace, but also to the joy of being reunited with those who have gone there before me, especially my dear wife, Ruth. The Bible says, 'Now we see but a poor reflection as in a mirror; then we shall see face to face' (1 Corinthians 13:12 NIV)."[243]

Richard Baxter. "I have pain—but I have peace; I have peace."[244]

John Knox. "Live in Christ, die in Christ, and the flesh need not fear death."[245]

Joseph Everett. "He said, 'GLORY! GLORY! GLORY!' and continued exclaiming 'GLORY!'" said Billy Graham, "for over twenty-five minutes until he entered Heaven."[246]

Augustus Toplady. "Oh! What delight! Who can fathom the joys of Heaven! I know it cannot be long now until my Savior will come for me." And then bursting into a flood of tears, he said, "All is light, light, light, light, the brightness of His own glory. Oh, come, Lord Jesus, come. Come quickly!"[247]

Blumbardt. Moments before death he exclaimed, "Light breaks in! Hallelujah!"

Olympia Morata. Dying, he said, "I distinctly behold a place filled with ineffable [inexpressible] light."

Stephen (disciple of Jesus). "Lord, lay not this sin to their charge" (Acts 7:60).

Lambert (a martyr under Henry VIII, while being consumed by a slow fire). "None but Christ; none but Christ!"[248]

Lawrence Saunders (martyred by the "bloody Queen Mary"). "Welcome the cross of Christ! Welcome the cross of Christ! Welcome life everlasting!"[249]

James Durham (to a friend). "For all that I have preached and written, there is but one Scripture that I can think of or dare to lay hold of. Tell me, brother, if I may dare lay the weight of my salvation on it: 'Whoever comes unto me, I will in no wise cast out!'"[250]

Doddridge. "I am full of confidence. There is a hope set before me; I have fled, I still fly for refuge to that hope. In Him I trust. In Him I have strong consolation and shall assuredly be accepted in the beloved of my soul."[251]

Thomas Scott (the commentator). "Lord, support me! Lord Jesus, receive my spirit! Christ is my all! He is my only hope! Oh, to realize the fullness of joy! Oh, to be done with temptation! This is

Heaven begun! I am done with darkness forever! Satan is vanquished! Nothing remains but salvation with eternal glory, eternal glory!"[252]

David Brainerd. "Oh! why is the chariot so long in coming? Why tarry the wheels of his chariot? Come, Lord Jesus; come, quickly!"[253]

Susanna Wesley. "Children, when I am gone, sing a song of praise to God."

Adoniram Judson. "I am not tired of my work; neither am I tired of the world; yet when Christ calls me home, I shall go with the gladness of a boy bounding away from school."

Charles Wesley. "I shall be satisfied with thy likeness—satisfied, satisfied!"

79. What Have the Lost Said at Death's Door?

Just as the last words of the saved are jubilant and hopeful, the last words of the unsaved are horrifying and hopeless.

Mirabeau. "Give me more laudanum, that I may not think of eternity."

Charles IX. "What blood, what murders, what evil counsels have I followed? I am lost! I see it well."

Thomas Hobbes (an atheist). "I am about to take a fearful leap in the dark."

Edward Gibbon. "All is dark and doubtful!"

Sir Francis Newport. "Oh, that I was to lie a thousand years upon the fire that never is quenched, to purchase the favor of God and be united to Him again! But it is a fruitless wish. Millions and millions of years would bring me no nearer to the end of my torments than one poor hour. Oh, eternity, eternity! Forever and forever! Oh, the insufferable pains of Hell!"

Lord Byron. "My days are in the yellow leaf; the flower and fruit of life are gone. The worm, the canker, and the grief are mine alone."

Sir Thomas Scott. "Until this moment I thought there was neither a God nor a Hell. Now I know and feel that there are both, and I am doomed to perdition by the just judgment of the Almighty."

J. H. Huxley (the great skeptic, looking up at some sight invisible to mortal eyes). "So it is true."

Brown. "Devils are in the room ready to drag my soul down to Hell! It's no use looking to Jesus now; it's too late!"

Adams (an infidel). "I'm lost! Lost! Lost! I'm damned! Damned! Damned forever!"

Kay (with a terror indescribable). "Hell! Hell!" (It is said that the terror in his words was so wrenching that his family had to flee the house until it passed.)

What will your last words be? Will they be words of triumph and joy with the saints or of utter despair and doom with the lost?

80. Will You Meet Me at the "Fountain" in Heaven?

At an industrial exposition in Chicago years ago a fountain became the meeting place for friends. Friends would say to one another, "Will you meet me at the fountain?" The answer was, "All right, I will meet you at the fountain."

P. P. Bliss was inspired to write a hymn based upon the fountain. Imagine a parent, spouse, sibling or friend saying,

Will you meet me at the fountain
　　When I reach the Gloryland?
When you meet me at the fountain
　　Shall I clasp your friendly hand?

Other friends will give you welcome,
　　Other loving voices cheer;
There'll be music at the fountain—
　　Will you, will you meet me there?

May you answer
Yes, I'll meet you at the fountain,
　　At the fountain bright and fair.
Oh, I'll meet you at the fountain;
　　Yes, I'll meet you, meet you there. ~ Philip Bliss (1873)

A wealthy man, upon hearing the unexpected news of his impending death, immediately called for his lawyer to form a will. The man willed this and that of his possessions away. To his wife and child, he instructed the lawyer to will their home. The man's child didn't understand death and said, "Papa, have you got a home in that Land you are going to?" The father's heart was smitten, but sadly too late, over failure to make arrangements for a new home beyond the grave.

Have you made the preparation for "moving day," when you will forever say farewell to your home here? Will you meet family and friends and me at the fountain?

In ancient Palestine men would use the ground as a bank to hide coins and other valuables. With that background in mind, Jesus said that the Kingdom of Heaven is like a man that upon discovering a vast treasure in a field sold all he had in order to purchase it (Matthew 13:44). The point of the parable is that Heaven is a treasure that is worth the exchange of every earthly possession, pleasure and pursuit to gain. It is worth any and every sacrifice to enter.

If you have not made the great exchange and experienced the transforming change that Christ freely gives upon your confession of sin and trust in Him, then do so now. "For what shall it profit a man, if he shall gain the whole world, and lose his own soul? Or what shall a man give in exchange for his soul?" (Mark 8:36–37).

> When the time shall come, fixed by irreversible decree, there shall be heard "a great voice from Heaven" to every believer in Christ, saying, "Come up hither." ~ C. H. Spurgeon

"When the time shall come, fixed by irreversible decree, there shall be heard 'a great voice from Heaven' to every believer in Christ, saying 'Come up hither' (Revelation 11:12)."[254] Anticipate it. Prepare for it. Welcome it. Go with it. Upon hearing the Lord say, "Come up hither," "all of earth's troubles will recede into utter insignificance. All our labors will be over, all our tears will be dried, and there will be nothing left but the sheer bliss of Heaven and our perfect enjoyment of God—forever."[255] If you are a Christian, you have the B.A. degree (Born-Again) which was given by God freely and fully based upon nothing else than repentance of sin and faith in and confession of Jesus Christ as Lord and Savior (John 3:3; Acts 20:21). Now strive to receive the W.D. (Well-Done) degree upon graduation from life to Heaven. Live so that Christ will greet you with the honorable commendation at life's end: "Well done, good and faithful servant...enter thou into the joy of thy lord" (Matthew 25:23).

Lord Jesus! When we think of Thee,
Of all Thy love and grace,
Our spirits long and fain would see
Thy beauty face to face.

Our Lord, our Life, our Rest, our Shield,
Our Rock, our Food, our Light—
Each thought of Thee doth constant yield
Unchanging, fresh delight.

Blest Savior, keep our spirits stayed
Hard following after Thee,
Till we, in robes of white arrayed,
Thy face in glory see. ~ James G. Deck (1881)

Somewhere there is a piece of statuary named "The Blind Watcher." It recounts the story of a young woman's sweetheart that had made a journey across the sea. Each evening, as the sun went down, she went to the seashore to watch for his return. Her father objected to her relationship with the young man and the daily watches. Upset with the relationship and the daily watches, in a fit of rage, he struck her across the face blinding her. Nonetheless, every evening she would go to the seashore. She couldn't look for him so she listened for him. He never returned. The young woman died "listening" for his return.[256] What tremendous love for and devotion to him possessed her!

With equal devotion, love, persistency and expectation ought we to look and listen for Jesus' return. He really is coming again!

115

And in that moment when He comes, may you join the saints that will be *"Caught Up to Heaven."*

ENDNOTES

[1] Lewis, C. S. *Mere Christianity*. (New York: HarperOne, 2001), 134.

[2] Criswell, W. A., P. Patterson, E. R. Clendenen, D. L. Akin, M. Chamberlin, D. K. Patterson, and J. Pogue, (Eds.). *Believer's Study Bible* (electronic ed.). (Nashville: Thomas Nelson, 1991), Rev. 21:1–22:5.

[3] Simeon, C. *Horae Homileticae: John XIII to Acts* (Vol. 14). (London: Holdsworth and Ball, 1833), 23.

[4] Criswell, W. A. *What to Do Until Jesus Comes Back*. (Nashville: Broadman Press, 1975), 24.

[5] Ibid.

[6] Addison, Joseph. *ADDISON: Selection From Addison's Papers Contributed to the Spectator*. (Oxford: Clarendon Press, 1875), 185.

[7] Ritzema, E., and E. Vince, (Eds.). *300 Quotations for Preachers from the Puritans*. (Bellingham, WA: Lexham Press, 2013).

[8] Spurgeon, C. H. *Morning and Evening*. (Grand Rapids: Zondervan Publishing House, 1969), April 20.

[9] MacArthur, John. *The Glory of Heaven*. (Nashville: Crossway, 2013), 80.

[10] Vines, Jerry. *Exploring 1. 2. 3. John*. (Neptune, NJ: Loizeaux Brothers, 1989), 186.

[11] Gangel, K. O. *John* (Vol. 4). (Nashville, TN: Broadman & Holman Publishers, 2000), 262.

[12] Graham, Franklin with Donna Lee Toney. *Billy Graham in Quotes*. (Nashville: Thomas Nelson, 2011), 170.

[13] Wuest, K. S. *Wuest's Word Studies from the Greek New Testament: for the English Reader* (Vol. 17) (Grand Rapids: Eerdmans, 1997), 49.

[14] Simeon, C. *Horae Homileticae: John XIII to Acts* (Vol. 14). (London: Holdsworth and Ball, 1833), 23.

[15] https://www.goodreads.com/quotes/234479-if-you-are-a-christian-you-are-not-a-citizen, accessed March 28, 2020.

[16] Bunyan, J. *Bunyan's Dying Sayings* (Vol. 1). (Bellingham, WA: Logos Bible Software, 2006), 66.

[17] Rice, John R. *Bible Facts About Heaven*. (Murfreesboro, TN: Sword of the Lord Publishers, 1940), Chapter 1.

[18] Criswell, W. A., P. Patterson, E. R. Clendenen, D. L. Akin, M. Chamberlin, D. K. Patterson, and J. Pogue, (Eds.). *Believer's Study Bible* (electronic ed.). (Nashville: Thomas Nelson, 1991), Rev. 21:1–22:5.

[19] Lewis, C. S. *The Great Divorce*. (New York: HarperCollins, 2001), 75.

[20] Morris, L. L. "Heaven." in D. R. W. Wood, I. H. Marshall, A. R. Millard, J. I. Packer, and D. J. Wiseman (Eds.). *New Bible Dictionary* (3rd ed.). (Leicester, England; Downers Grove, IL: InterVarsity Press, 1996), 457.

[21] Exell, J. S. *The Biblical Illustrator: The Psalms* (Vol. 1). (New York; Chicago; Toronto; London; Edinburgh: Fleming H. Revell Company; Francis Griffiths, 1909), 265.

[22] Jones, G. C. *1000 Illustrations for Preaching and Teaching*. (Nashville, TN: Broadman & Holman Publishers, 1986), 148.

[23] Exell, J. S. *The Biblical Illustrator: St. John* (Vol. 2). (London: James Nisbet & Co., 1909), 473.

[24] Pink, A. W. *Exposition of the Gospel of John*. (Swengel, PA: Bible Truth Depot, 1923–1945), 757.

[25] Jamieson, R., A. R. Fausset, and D. Brown. *Commentary Critical and Explanatory on the Whole Bible* (Vol. 2). (Oak Harbor, WA: Logos Research Systems, Inc., 1997), 156.

[26] https://www.christianitytoday.com/history/people/poets/fanny-crosby.html, accessed April 1, 2020.

[27] Hutson, Curtis. (Ed.). *Great Preaching on Heaven*. (Murfreesboro, TN: Sword of the Lord Publishers, 1989), 107.

ENDNOTES

[28] Exell, J. S. *The Biblical Illustrator: St. John* (Vol. 2). (London: James Nisbet & Co., 1909), 480

[29] Rice, John R. *Bible Facts About Heaven*. (Murfreesboro, TN: Sword of the Lord Publishers, 1940), Chapter 2.

[30] Tozer, A. W. "Mornings with Tozer" (Devotional). http://www.sermonindex.net/modules/ newbb/viewtopic.php?topic_id=47045&forum=45, accessed April 6, 2020.

[31] Granted these words are not in reference to Heaven, but Heavenly wisdom. Nonetheless, no harm or biblical injustice is done to apply them to Heaven, for that which they state is expressly true of that glorious City.

[32] Courson, Jon. *Jon Courson's Application Commentary*. (Nashville: Thomas Nelson, 2003), 555.

[33] Gangel, K. O. *John* (Vol. 4). (Nashville, TN: Broadman & Holman Publishers, 2000), 264.

[34] ibid.

[35] Carson, D. A. *The Gospel According to John*. (Leicester, England; Grand Rapids, MI: Inter-Varsity Press; W.B. Eerdmans, 1991), 489.

[36] Pink, A. W. *Exposition of the Gospel of John*. (Swengel, PA: Bible Truth Depot, 1923–1945), 759.

[37] Whitlock, L. G., R. C. Sproul, B. K. Waltke, and M. Silva. *The Reformation Study Bible: Bringing the Light of the Reformation to Scripture: New King James Version*. (Nashville: T. Nelson, 1995), John 14:2.

[38] Hutson, Curtis. (Ed.). *Great Preaching on Heaven*. (Murfreesboro, TN: Sword of the Lord Publishers, 1989), 20.

[39] Ibid., 235.

[40] Criswell, W. A. and Paige Patterson, *Heaven*. (Grand Rapids: Tyndale House Publishers, 1991), 34.

[41] Ibid., 42.

[42] Stanford, C. *The Biblical Illustrator.* "The Nearness of Heaven." Hebrews 6:17–20.

[43] Graham, B. *The Heaven Answer Book.* (Nashville: Thomas Nelson, 2012).

[44] Tan, P. L. *Encyclopedia of 7700 Illustrations: Signs of the Times.* (Garland, TX: Bible Communications, Inc., 1996), 545.

[45] Beecher, Henry Ward. *Life Thoughts: Gathered from the Extemporaneous Discourses of Henry Ward Beecher.* (New York: Sheldon and Company, 1869), 176.

[46] Morgan, R. J. *Nelson's Complete Book of Stories, Illustrations, and Quotes* (electronic ed.). (Nashville: Thomas Nelson Publishers, 2000), 426.

[47] A Sermon by C. H. Spurgeon Delivered on Sunday Morning, August 9, 1868, at the Metropolitan Tabernacle, Newington.

[48] Radmacher, E. D., R. B. Allen, and H. W. House, *The Nelson Study Bible: New King James Version.* (Nashville: T. Nelson Publishers, 1997), Jude 24–25.

[49] Henry, M. *Matthew Henry Commentary on the Whole Bible: Complete and Unabridged in One Volume.* (Peabody: Hendrickson, 1994), 2463.

[50] Spurgeon, C. H. *Morning and Evening.* (Grand Rapids: Zondervan Publishing House, 1969), October 10.

[51] Criswell, W. A., P. Patterson, E. R. Clendenen, D. L. Akin, M. Chamberlin, D. K. Patterson, and J. Pogue, (Eds.). *Believer's Study Bible* (electronic ed.). (Nashville: Thomas Nelson, 1991), John 14:2.

[52] Simeon, C. *Horae Homileticae: John XIII to Acts* (Vol. 14). (London: Holdsworth and Ball, 1833), 23.

[53] Pink, A. W. *Exposition of the Gospel of John.* (Swengel, PA: Bible Truth Depot, 1923–1945), 758.

[54] Rice, John R. The Gospel of John. (Murfreesboro, TN: Sword of the Lord Publishers, 1976), 275.

ENDNOTES

[55] Henry, M. *Matthew Henry Commentary on the Whole Bible: Complete and Unabridged in One Volume.* (Peabody: Hendrickson, 2008), John 14:2.

[56] McGee, J. V. *Thru the Bible Commentary: The Gospels (Luke),* (electronic ed., Vol. 37). (Nashville: Thomas Nelson, 1991), 267.

[57] Edwards, Jonathan. "Many Mansions." www.biblebb.com/files/edwards/JE-mansions.htm, accessed April 21, 2011.

[58] Tan, P. L. *Encyclopedia of 7700 Illustrations: Signs of the Times.* (Garland, TX: Bible Communications, Inc., 1996), 312.

[59] Cabal, T., C. O. Brand, E. R. Clendenen, P. Copan, J. P. Moreland, and D. Powell. *The Apologetics Study Bible: Real Questions, Straight Answers, Stronger Faith.* (Nashville, TN: Holman Bible Publishers, 2007), 1732.

[60] Wiersbe, W. W. *Wiersbe's Expository Outlines on the New Testament.* (Wheaton, IL: Victor Books, 1992), 467.

[61] MacDonald, W., A. Farstad, (Ed.). *Believer's Bible Commentary: Old and New Testaments.* (Nashville: Thomas Nelson, 1995), 1353.

[62] MacArthur, John, Jr., (Ed.). The John MacArthur Study Bible (electronic ed.). (Nashville, TN: Word Pub., 1997), 1757.

[63] Courson, Jon. *Jon Courson's Application Commentary.* (Nashville: Thomas Nelson, 2003), 1090.

[64] Graham, Franklin with Donna Lee Toney. *Billy Graham in Quotes.* (Nashville: Thomas Nelson, 2011), 171.

[65] MacDonald, W., A. Farstad, (Ed.). *Believer's Bible Commentary: Old and New Testaments.* (Nashville: Thomas Nelson, 1995), 1977.

[66] Spurgeon, C. H. *The Complete Works of C. H. Spurgeon,* Volume 14: Sermons 788 to 847.

[67] MacLaren, Alexander. *MacLaren Expositions of Holy Scripture*, St. John, Chaps. IX to XIV. (Grand Rapids: Baker Book House, 1977), 265.

[68] Henry, M. *Matthew Henry Commentary on the Whole Bible: Complete and Unabridged in One Volume.* (Peabody: Hendrickson, 1994), 1214.

[69] Graham, B. *The Heaven Answer Book.* (Nashville: Thomas Nelson, 2012), 115.

[70] MacDonald, W., A. Farstad, (Ed.). *Believer's Bible Commentary: Old and New Testaments.* (Nashville: Thomas Nelson, 1995), 2379.

[71] MacArthur, John, Jr., (Ed.). The John MacArthur Study Bible (electronic ed.). (Nashville, TN: Word Pub., 1997), 2002.

[72] Walvoord, J. F. "Revelation," in J. F. Walvoord and R. B. Zuck (Eds.), *The Bible Knowledge Commentary: An Exposition of the Scriptures* (Vol. 2). (Wheaton, IL: Victor Books, 1985), 985.

[73] Kistemaker, Simon J. *Revelation: New Testament Commentary.* (Grand Rapids: Baker Academic, 2001), 558.

[74] Spurgeon, C. H. "Heaven and Hell" (sermon), preached September 4, 1855, New Park Street.

[75] Bunyan, J. *Bunyan's Dying Sayings* (Vol. 1). (Bellingham, WA: Logos Bible Software, 2006), 66.

[76] MacArthur, John. *The Glory of Heaven.* (Nashville: Crossway, 2013), 13.

[77] Ibid.

[78] Ibid.

[79] Hodge, C. *Systematic Theology* (Vol. 3). (Oak Harbor, WA: Logos Research Systems, Inc., 1997), 750.

[80] Stewart, R. "Purgatory," in C. Brand, C. Draper, A. England, S. Bond, E. R. Clendenen, and T. C. Butler (Eds.). *Holman Illustrated Bible Dictionary.* (Nashville, TN: Holman Bible Publishers, 2003), 1350.

[81] Graham, B. *The Heaven Answer Book.* (Nashville: Thomas Nelson, 2012).

[82] MacArthur, John. *The Glory of Heaven.* (Nashville: Crossway, 2013), 18.

[83] Spurgeon, C. H. *New Park Street Pulpit* (6 Volumes). (London: Passmore & Alabaster, 1856), "Heaven" (a sermon) preached December 16, 1855.

[84] MacArthur, John. *The Glory of Heaven.* (Nashville: Crossway, 2013), 18.

[85] Graham, B. *The Heaven Answer Book.* (Nashville: Thomas Nelson, 2012).

ENDNOTES

[86] Jones, G. C. *1000 Illustrations for Preaching and Teaching*. (Nashville, TN: Broadman & Holman Publishers, 1986), 151.

[87] Henry, M. *Matthew Henry Commentary on the Whole Bible: Complete and Unabridged in One Volume*. (Peabody: Hendrickson, 1994), 1214.

[88] Swindoll, Chuck. Insight for Today: The Reality of Heaven. December 14, 2017.

[89] Criswell, W. A. and Paige Patterson, *Heaven*. (Grand Rapids: Tyndale House Publishers, 1991), 33.

[90] Wiersbe, W. W. *With the Word Bible Commentary*. (Nashville: Thomas Nelson, 1991), Revelation 7:1.

[91] Herschel Ford. *Simple Sermons on Heaven, Hell, and Judgment*. (Grand Rapids: Zondervan, 1969), 26.

[92] Criswell, W. A. and Paige Patterson, *Heaven*. (Grand Rapids: Tyndale House Publishers, 1991), 33.

[93] Tozer, A. W. "The Bliss of Heaven." The Alliance Tozer Devotional. https://www.cmalliance. org/devotions/tozer?id=1401, accessed April 6, 2020.

[94] Henry, M. *Matthew Henry Commentary on the Whole Bible: Complete and Unabridged in One Volume*. (Peabody: Hendrickson, 1994), 954.

[95] From Martin Luther's *Table Talk*.

[96] *The Westminster Presbyterian Journal*. (Philadelphia, PA: The Holmes Press, December 4, 1909), 15.

[97] John MacArthur. Grace to You. Will There Be Any Sin or Sorrow in Heaven?, https://www.gty. org/library/questions/QA107/will-there-be-any-sin-or-sorrow-in-Heaven, accessed March 24, 2020.

[98] Exell, J. S. *The Biblical Illustrator: The Psalms* (Vol. 1). (New York; Chicago; Toronto; London; Edinburgh: Fleming H. Revell Company; Francis Griffiths, 1909), 264.

[99] Radmacher, E. D., R. B. Allen, and H. W. House. *Nelson's New Illustrated Bible Commentary*. (Nashville: T. Nelson Publishers, 1999), 1765.

[100] Horne, G. *A Commentary on the Book of Psalms.* (New York: Robert Carter & Brothers, 1856), 501.

[101] Wiersbe, W. W. *With the Word Bible Commentary.* (Nashville: Thomas Nelson, 1991), Psalm 48:1.

[102] Ironside, H. A. *Lectures on the Book of Revelation.* (Neptune, N. J.: Loizeaux Brothers, 1920), 83.

[103] ibid.

[104] Ibid., 82.

[105] Henry, M. *Matthew Henry Commentary on the Whole Bible: Complete and Unabridged in One Volume.* (Peabody: Hendrickson, 1994), Revelation 4:10.

[106] Clarke, Adam. Commentary on the Bible. (1831), Revelation 4:10.

[107] *The Cambridge Bible for Schools and Colleges,* Revelation 4:10.

[108] Jamieson, Robert, A. R. Fausset and David Brown. *A Commentary, Critical, Practical, and Explanatory on the Old and New Testaments.* (1882), Revelation 4:10.

[109] Ironside, H. A. *Eternal Security of the Believer.* (Neptune, New Jersey: Loizeaux Brothers, 1934), 8.

[110] Spurgeon, C. H. "The Holdfast" (sermon No. 1418), June 9th, 1878. www.biblebb.com/files/ spurgeon/1418.htm, accessed December 27, 2014.

[111] Barna Research. "Americans Describe Their Views About Life After Death." https://www. barna.com/research/americans-describe-their-views-about-life-after-death/, accessed April 2, 2020.

[112] Spurgeon, C. H. "Faith in Perfection" (a sermon). www.C. H. Spurgeon.org, accessed April 2, 2020.

[113] Christopher W. Morgan and Robert A. Peterson, (Ed.). *Is Hell for Real or Does Everyone Go to Heaven?* (Grand Rapids: Zondervan, 2011), 64–65.

[114] Ibid., 66.

[115] Tozer, A. W. "Infinite Equity," (Devotional). September 12, 2014. https://www.cmalliance.org/ devotions/tozer?id=1400, accessed December 13, 2014.

[116] Hutson, Curtis. (Ed.). *Great Preaching on Heaven*. (Murfreesboro, TN: Sword of the Lord Publishers, 1989), 15.

[117] Watson, Thomas. "A Believer's Last Day, His Best Day," (sermon excerpt). http://www. christianitytoday.com/ch/thepastinthepresent/classicfaithformoderntimes/abe lieverslastday.html?start=1, accessed March 23, 2020.

[118] Hayford, J. W. (Ed.). *Spirit-Filled Life Study Bible* (electronic ed.). (Nashville, TN: Thomas Nelson, 1997), 1 Corinthians 15:51.

[119] MacArthur, John, Jr., (Ed.). The John MacArthur Study Bible (electronic ed.). (Nashville, TN: Word Pub., 1997), 1757.

[120] Wiersbe, W. W. *The Bible Exposition Commentary* (Vol. 1). (Wheaton, IL: Victor Books, 1996). 619.

[121] Criswell, W. A. *The Criswell Study Bible*. (Nashville: Thomas Nelson Publishing Company, 1979), 1459.

[122] Baucham, Voddie. *The Courier*. (Greenville, SC), Febuary, 2015, 6.

[123] Exell, J. S. *The Biblical Illustrator: St. John* (Vol. 2). (London: James Nisbet & Co., 1909), 465.

[124] Lloyd-Jones, D. M. *The Church and the Last Things*. (Wheaton, IL: Crossway Books, 1998), 64.

[125] Exell, J. S. *The Biblical Illustrator: St. John* (Vol. 2). (London: James Nisbet & Co., 1909), 473.

[126] Tan, P. L. *Encyclopedia of 7700 Illustrations: Signs of the Times*. (Garland, TX: Bible Communications, Inc., 1996), 545–546.

[127] Exell, J. S. *The Biblical Illustrator: St. John* (Vol. 2). (London: James Nisbet & Co., 1909), 477.

128 Enduring Word. "Hebrews 12—Reasons to Endure Discouraging Times." https:// enduringword.com/bible-commentary/hebrews-12/, accessed March 24, 2020.

129 Wuest, K. S. *Wuest's Word Studies from the Greek New Testament: for the English Reader* (Vol. 17) (Grand Rapids: Eerdmans, 1997), Heb. 12:1.

130 Hagner, Donald A. *New International Biblical Commentary.* (Carlisle, PA: Hendrickson Publishers, 1990), 211.

131 MacArthur, John, Jr., (Ed.). The John MacArthur Study Bible (electronic ed.). (Nashville, TN: Word Pub., 1997), 1919.

132 Hacking, P. H. *Opening Up Hebrews.* (Leominster: Day One Publications, 2006), 82.

133 Wiersbe, W. W. Wiersbe's Expository Outlines on the New Testament. (Wheaton, IL: Victor Books, 1992), 710.

134 MacDonald, W., A. Farstad, (Ed.). *Believer's Bible Commentary: Old and New Testaments.* (Nashville: Thomas Nelson, 1995), 2002.

135 Graham, B. *The Heaven Answer Book.* (Nashville: Thomas Nelson, 2012).

136 Exell, J. S. *The Biblical Illustrator: St. Luke* (Vol. III). (London: Francis Griffiths, 1904), 79.

137 Henry, M. *Matthew Henry Commentary on the Whole Bible: Complete and Unabridged in One Volume.* (Peabody: Hendrickson, 1994), 456.

138 MacArthur, John, Jr., (Ed.). The John MacArthur Study Bible (electronic ed.). (Nashville, TN: Word Pub., 1997), 444.

139 Spurgeon, C. H. *2,200 Quotations from the Writings of Charles Spurgeon: Arranged Topically or Textually and Indexed by Subject, Scripture, and People.* (T. Carter, Ed.) (Grand Rapids, MI: Baker Books, 1995), 95.

140 Henry, M. *Matthew Henry Commentary on the Whole Bible: Complete and Unabridged in One Volume.* (Peabody: Hendrickson, 1994), 456.

141 Ibid., 456.

ENDNOTES

[142] Peabody, W. B. O. *The Biblical Illustrator.* "We Know in Part," 1 Corinthians 13:12.

[143] Ellingworth, P., H. Hatton, and P. Ellingworth. *A Handbook on Paul's First Letter to the Corinthians.* (New York: United Bible Societies, 1995), 300.

[144] Robertson, A. T. *Word Pictures in the New Testament.* (Nashville, TN: Broadman Press, 1933), 1 Corinthians 13:12.

[145] Barnes, Albert. *Barnes Notes on the Bible,* 1 Corinthians 13:9.

[146] Exell, J. S. *The Biblical Illustrator: The Psalms* (Vol. 1). (New York; Chicago; Toronto; London; Edinburgh: Fleming H. Revell Company; Francis Griffiths, 1909), 265.

[147] Hutson, Curtis. (Ed.). *Great Preaching on Heaven.* (Murfreesboro, TN: Sword of the Lord Publishers, 1989), 104.

[148] Ibid.

[149] Exell, J. S. *The Biblical Illustrator: The Psalms* (Vol. 1). (New York; Chicago; Toronto; London; Edinburgh: Fleming H. Revell Company; Francis Griffiths, 1909), 263.

[150] Spurgeon, C. H. "And They Shall See His Face," sermon delivered on Sunday morning, August 9, 1868, The Metropolitan Tabernacle, Newington.

[151] Allen, Kerry James. *Exploring the Mind & Heart of the Prince of Preachers.* (Oswego, IL: Fox River Press, 2005), 217.

[152] Yancy, Phillip. *Two Books in One: What's So Amazing About Grace and Where is God when it Hurts.* (Grand Rapids: Zondervan, 2009).

[153] MacArthur, John. *The Glory of Heaven.* (Nashville: Crossway, 2013), 84.

[154] MacArthur, John. *The Glory of Heaven.* (Nashville: Crossway, 2013), 84.

[155] Little, Paul E. *Know What You Believe.* (Wheaton: Victor Books, 1979), 189.

[156] Courson, Jon. *Jon Courson's Application Commentary.* (Nashville: Thomas Nelson, 2003), 556.

[157] Exell, J. S. *The Biblical Illustrator: The Psalms* (Vol. 1). (New York; Chicago; Toronto; London; Edinburgh: Fleming H. Revell Company; Francis Griffiths, 1909), 272.

[158] Graham, Billy. "Billy Graham Answers," June 21, 2012.

[159] ibid.

[160] Tozer, A. W. "Model Christians," Devotional: June 13, 2020. https://www.cmalliance.org/ devotions/tozer?id=372, accessed April 9, 2020.

[161] *Love Worth Finding*—Mar. 14, 2009. https://www.crosswalk.com/devotionals/ loveworthfinding/love-worth-finding-mar-14-2009-11600625.html, accessed March 28, 2020.

[162] Baxter, Richard. *The Saints' Everlasting Rest,* abridged by John T. Wilkinson. (London: Epworth, 1962), 110.

[163] Packer, J. I. (1993). Introduction. In Psalms (p. 287). Wheaton, IL: Crossway Books.

[164] Baxter, Richard. *The Saints' Everlasting Rest,* paraphrase and abridgment by Robert E. Baxter. (1652), https://www.gracegems.org/book4/Baxter.htm, accessed March 28, 2020.

[165] Addison, Joseph. *ADDISON: Selection From Addison's Papers Contributed to the Spectator.* (Oxford: Clarendon Press, 1875), 184.

[166] Simeon, C. *Horae Homileticae: John XIII to Acts* (Vol. 14). (London: Holdsworth and Ball, 1833), 25.

[167] MacDonald, W., A. Farstad, (Ed.). *Believer's Bible Commentary: Old and New Testaments.* (Nashville: Thomas Nelson, 1995), 2007.

[168] Lewis, C. S. *Mere Christianity.* (New York: HarperOne, 2001), 57.

[169] The author adapted points cited from Richard Baxter's book *The Saints' Everlasting Rest: How to Seek the Saints' Rest on Earth.* Additional points are original.

[170] Lewis, C. S. *The Problem of Pain.* (New York: Harper One, 1996), 149.

ENDNOTES

171 Ritzema, E., and E. Vince, (Eds.). *300 Quotations for Preachers from the Puritans*. (Bellingham, WA: Lexham Press, 2013).

172 Hutson, Curtis. (Ed.). *Great Preaching on Heaven*. (Murfreesboro, TN: Sword of the Lord Publishers, 1989), 237.

173 Graham, Franklin with Donna Lee Toney. *Billy Graham in Quotes*. (Nashville: Thomas Nelson, 2011), 171.

174 Henry, M. *Matthew Henry Commentary on the Whole Bible: Complete and Unabridged in One Volume*. (Peabody: Hendrickson, 1994), 814.

175 Simeon, C. *Horae Homileticae: Psalms, LXXIII–CL* (Vol. 6). (London: Samuel Holdsworth, 1836), 291).

176 Spurgeon, C. H. *Morning and Evening*. (Grand Rapids: Zondervan Publishing House, 1969), April 8.

177 Rice, John R. The Gospel of John. (Murfreesboro, TN: Sword of the Lord Publishers, 1976), 276.

178 Phillips, John. *Exploring the Gospel of John*. (Grand Rapids: Kregal Publications, 1989), 263. [The author paraphrased John Phillips' words, entire paragraph].

179 Spurgeon, C. H. *Morning and Evening*. (Grand Rapids: Zondervan Publishing House, 1969), November 17 (Evening).

180 L. B. Cowman. *Streams in the Desert,* Updated Edition. (Grand Rapids: Zondervan, 1977), 232.

181 Criswell, W. A. and Paige Patterson, *Heaven*. (Grand Rapids: Tyndale House Publishers, 1991), 121.

182 Stanley, Charles. *Handbook on Christian Living,* 272–273.

183 Criswell, W. A. "What I Believe about Heaven: The Inexpressible Preciousness," sermon. June 24, 1990.

184 https://www.goodreads.com/quotes/99178-god-is-the-highest-good-of-the-reasonable-creature-the, accessed March 29, 2020.

[185] Henry, Matthew. *An Exposition of the Old and New Testament.* (London: Joseph Robinson, 1839), 873.

[186] https://www.inspiringquotes.us/author/6376-john-r-rice, Accessed March 29, 2020.

[187] MacDonald, W., A. Farstad, (Ed.). *Believer's Bible Commentary: Old and New Testaments.* (Nashville: Thomas Nelson, 2016), 759.

[188] Grassmick, J. D. "Mark," in J. F. Walvoord and R. B. Zuck (Eds.), *The Bible Knowledge Commentary: An Exposition of the Scriptures* (Vol. 2). (Wheaton, IL: Victor Books, 1985), 163.

[189] Hobbs, H. H. *My Favorite Illustrations.* (Nashville, TN: Broadman Press, 1990), 133.

[190] McGee, J. V. *Thru the Bible Commentary: The Gospels (Mark),* (electronic ed., Vol. 36). (Nashville: Thomas Nelson, 1991), 147.

[191] Berkhof, Louis. *Systematic Theology*, 403. https://www.wtsbooks.com/products/systematic-theology-louis-berkhof-9780802876324?variant=9801499050031, accessed April 17, 2020.

[192] M'Cheyne, Robert Murray. http://www.mcheyne.info/quotes/, accessed April 17, 2020.

[193] Barnes, Albert. *Barnes Notes on the Bible*, Hebrews 7:25.

[194] *Calvin's Commentaries.* "A Harmony of the Gospels," (Baker), 3:313.

[195] Wuest, K. S. *Wuest's Word Studies from the Greek New Testament: for the English Reader* (Vol. 17) (Grand Rapids: Eerdmans, 1997), 32.

[196] Source unknown.

[197] Spurgeon, C. H. *Morning and Evening.* (Grand Rapids: Zondervan Publishing House, 1969), October 3.

[198] Graham, Billy. "Billy Graham Answers," June 21, 2012.

ENDNOTES

[199] Hayford, J. W. (Ed.). *Spirit-Filled Life Study Bible* (electronic ed.). (Nashville, TN: Thomas Nelson, 1997), Hebrews 1:7.

[200] ibid.

[201] MacDonald, W., A. Farstad, (Ed.). *Believer's Bible Commentary: Old and New Testaments.* (Nashville: Thomas Nelson, 1995), 2161.

[202] Spence-Jones, H. D. M. (Ed.). *Hebrews.* (London; New York: Funk & Wagnalls Company, 1909), 30.

[203] ibid.

[204] Jeremiah, David. "Your Heavenly Escorts," *Turning Point.* https://www.oneplace.com/ ministries/turning-point/read/articles/your-Heavenly-escorts-16251.html, accessed March 30, 2020.

[205] Spurgeon, C. H. *Morning and Evening.* (Grand Rapids: Zondervan Publishing House, 1969), October 3.

[206] Exell, J. S. *The Biblical Illustrator: Hebrews* (Vol. 1). (London: James Nisbet & Co, 1909), 64.

[207] Graham, Billy. *Angels, God's Secret Agents.* (Garden City, NY: Doubleday & Company, Inc., 1975), Back-cover.

[208] Exell, J. S. *The Biblical Illustrator: Hebrews* (Vol. 1). (London: James Nisbet & Co, 1909), 70–71.

[209] Ibid., 71.

[210] Graham, Billy. *Angels, God's Secret Agents.* (Garden City, NY: Doubleday & Company, Inc., 1975), 2–3.

[211] ibid., back cover.

[212] Courson, Jon. *Jon Courson's Application Commentary.* (Nashville: Thomas Nelson, 2003), 1438.

[213] Jenkins, Dave. "Are Demons Fallen Angels." https://www.christianity.com/wiki/angels-and-demons/are-demons-really-fallen-angels.html, accessed April 18, 2020.

[214] Taylor, Jack R. *Victory Over the Devil.* (Nashville: Broadman Press, 1973), 9.

[215] Sanders, J. Oswald. *The Divine Art of Soul Winning,* 40–41.

[216] Simeon, C. *Horae Homileticae: Revelation-Claude's Essay-Indexes* (Vol. 21). (London: Holdsworth and Ball, 1833), 174.

[217] Graham, Billy. *Angels, God's Secret Agents.* (Garden City, NY: Doubleday & Company, Inc., 1975), 98.

[218] Bunyan, J. *Bunyan's Dying Sayings* (Vol. 1). (Bellingham, WA: Logos Bible Software, 2006), 66.

[219] Beale, G. K. *The Book of Revelation: A Commentary on the Greek Text.* (Grand Rapids, MI; Carlisle, Cumbria: W.B. Eerdmans; Paternoster Press, 1999), 1112.

[220] MacArthur, John, Jr., (Ed.). The John MacArthur Study Bible (electronic ed.). (Nashville, TN: Word Pub., 1997), 2024.

[221] Exell, J. S. *The Biblical Illustrator: Revelation*. (London: James Nisbet & Co., 1909), 698.

[222] Wiersbe, W. W. Wiersbe's Expository Outlines on the New Testament. (Wheaton, IL: Victor Books, 1992), 819.

[223] Exell, J. S. The Biblical Illustrator: Second Corinthians (p. 258). New York; Chicago; Toronto: Fleming H. Revell Company.

[224] ibid., 260.

[225] Lewis, C. S. *The Weight of Glory.* (New York: HarperCollins, 1980), 47.

[226] Drummond, Lewis. Cited in Jack Smith. *Great Soul-Winning Motivational Sermons.* (Home Mission Board of the Southern Baptist Convention, 1994), 55.

[227] Tozer, A. W. "Heaven: A 28-Day Advent Devotional." https://www.goodreads.com/work/ quotes/48761527-from-Heaven-a-28-day-advent-devotional, accessed April 6, 2020.

[228] MacArthur, John. *The Glory of Heaven.* (Nashville: Crossway, 2013), 65.

[229] Hutson, Curtis. (Ed.). *Great Preaching on Heaven.* (Murfreesboro, TN: Sword of the Lord Publishers, 1989), 199–200.

ENDNOTES

230 Graham, B. *The Heaven Answer Book.* (Nashville: Thomas Nelson, 2012).

231 Maclaren, Alexander. *Expositions of Holy Scripture: Esther, Job, Proverbs, and Ecclesiastes.* (New York: Armstrong and Sons, 1908), 109.

232 Allen, Kerry James. *Exploring the Mind & Heart of the Prince of Preachers.* (Oswego, IL: Fox River Press, 2005), 214–215.

233 Rogers, Adrian. "What Heaven Is Like." https://www.lwf.org/questions-and-answers/what-is-Heaven-like, accessed March 28, 2020.

234 Henry, M. *Matthew Henry Commentary on the Whole Bible: Complete and Unabridged in One Volume.* (Peabody: Hendrickson, 1994), 2247.

235 MacLaren, Alexander. *MacLaren Expositions of Holy Scripture*, St. John, Chaps. IX to XIV. (Grand Rapids: Baker Book House, 1977), 271.

236 Ibid., 270–271.

237 Talmage, T. De Witt. "The Ferry Boat of the Jordan" (sermon). http://biblehub.com/sermons/ auth/talmage/the_ferry-boat_of_the_jordan.htm, accessed January 2, 2017.

238 Chambers, Oswald. *My Utmost for His Highest,* May 13.

239 Ironside, H. A. *Notes on the Book of Proverbs.* (Neptune, NJ: Loizeaux Brothers, 1908), 437.

240 Spurgeon, C. H. *New Park Street Pulpit,* Volume 1. "Thoughts on the Last Battle" (Sermon No. 23). May 13, 1855.

241 Barnes, Albert. *Barnes Notes on the Bible*, (1834).

242 The Sword of the Lord. "What the Saved Said at Death's Door and What the Lost Said at Death's Door." (Murfreesboro, TN: Sword of the Lord Publishers, August 11, 2006). Additional quotes from other sources.

243 Billy Graham's Last Column: "By the time you read this, I will be in Heaven." https://www. fayobserver.com/news/20180221/billy-grahams-last-column-by-time-you-read-this-i-will-be-in-Heaven, accessed March 22, 2020.

244 From Christianty.com, "Famous Last Words," accessed March 21, 2020.

245 Ibid.

[246] Ibid.

[247] MacArthur, John. The Solution to a Troubled Heart. http://www.gty.org, accessed May 22, 2013.

[248] https://www.gracegems.org/Books2/dh08.htm, accessed April 4, 2020.

[249] ibid.

[250] ibid.

[251] ibid.

[252] ibid.

[253] ibid.

[254] Hutson, Curtis. (Ed.). *Great Preaching on Heaven.* (Murfreesboro, TN: Sword of the Lord Publishers, 1989), 191.

[255] MacArthur, John. *The Glory of Heaven.* (Nashville: Crossway, 2013), 172.

[256] Herschel Ford. *Simple Sermons on Heaven, Hell, and Judgment.* (Grand Rapids: Zondervan, 1969), 91–92.

9 7 8 1 8 7 8 1 2 7 4 2 6